MESSAGE IN A BODY

BY JOSEPH ANFUSO

To Karen—the love of my life, and my best friend.

"We carry this precious Message around in the unadorned clay pots of our ordinary lives."

2 Corinthians 4:7 (msg)

What Others are Saying about *Message in a Body*

"This story of journey is common enough that we can each identify ourselves in these pages, and extraordinary enough that it will reach the quiet places in our hearts and call us upward."

— **William Paul Young, Author, The Shack**

"This is one powerful story! After growing up Roman Catholic, Joe Anfuso rejected the religion of his childhood—convinced that he was alone in the world. In *Message in a Body*, he honestly shares stories of his years of struggles with Eastern and Western religions before making an unexpected discovery that would change his life. *Message in a Body* is a touching and thrilling story of one man's journey to find God and answer His call to serve."

— **Richard Stearns, President, World Vision US**
Author, The Hole in Our Gospel

"If you, too, yearn to hear the words, "I love you...I love you...I love you" as you traverse life's rocky terrain, *Message in a Body* will touch your soul. Joe Anfuso provides a candid narrative of his own discovery of the relentless, ever-present, life-changing love of Christ, even while seeking his own unique life-calling. Against the backdrop of Joe's trek toward work among the poor, this account can convince other journeyers of God's sufficiency to meet anyone at any stage in their journey."

— **Benjamin K. Homan , President, Food for the Hungry**

"In Joe Anfuso's gentle and transparent way, he recounts his wanderings in search of truth and meaning in the tumultuous '60s and early '70s. It's a remarkable journey through changing spiritual, cultural and geographic landscapes which ultimately leads "home." In his eventual encounter with the truth he so stubbornly resisted, Joe finds answers that satisfy his roving intellect, love that fills his empty heart, and purpose that settles his heart-wrenching search for identity. Joe's account of how God lovingly and patiently brought him to his current place of leadership in an organization that today changes lives and impacts nations is a reassuring and powerful confirmation of Jesus' promise that if we seek (and keep on seeking!) we will find...not only truth, but meaning, purpose and identity – the pillars of life for which every created soul so desperately longs."

— **W. Ray Norman, Ph.D., Dean, School of Mathematics,**
Engineering and Business, Messiah College

"*Message in a Body* is a wonderful book. Joe Anfuso is a gifted visionary and servant-leader who writes the way he lives—with simplicity, clarity, and a passion for life. His fascinating story of privilege turned into purpose will powerfully inspire all who seek for the God who is already seeking us."

— **Kip Jacob, Senior Pastor, SouthLake Foursquare Church**

"If I didn't know Joe Anfuso personally, I wouldn't have believed his story. Tracing Joe's childhood as the son of a powerful New York congressman to his years of traveling through some of the roughest and most exotic regions on earth, *Message in a Body* reads like the screenplay of a movie—a unique mix of action-flick, romantic comedy and spiritual journey. As I read, I walked with Joe down the intriguing hallway of his memories (along with a cast of historic characters, including JFK) as he chronicled the inner pain and yearnings we all feel when we're listening to our souls. His vulnerability and honesty make you feel like you're not the only one who doubts on the inside, while searching for truth and meaning in the perplexing world that surrounds us all."

— **Chris Kainu, Lead Pastor, Summit View Church**

"What does it take to touch a heart with the message of God's love? The obtainable answer is revealed within the pages of this extraordinary book, filled with transparency, tenderness and the uncommon characteristic of compassion for the poor. Do you want to know the answer? Then devour this book by my friend of years, Joe Anfuso. Then you, too, will have a message in your body—one that will not only change your life, but possibly the world in which you live."

— **Dr. James W. Goll, Co-founder, Encounters Network**

Foreword

Ever since I first met Joseph Anfuso I have been impressed and challenged by his story. His unique life experience—filled with exotic travel and a thirst for knowledge—has always intrigued and encouraged me. His firsthand knowledge of world religions, his ever-present desire for authentic living, his passion for the world's hurting and genuine love for people is a challenge to us all.

There is much in Joseph's story with which I can identify. We are both twins. We are both sons of famous, successful fathers. We are both leaders of non-profit organizations in the Portland, Oregon area. We have done work together. We have ministered together. We have dreamed together.

Quite frankly, before reading this book I thought I knew Joseph fairly well. And in a certain way, I did. But reading the full story of what has made him the person he is today—his depth of experience, understanding, wisdom and knowledge—has added a whole new dimension and appreciation for Joseph. Learning about his experiences in India, Nepal and Afghanistan…hearing of the pain and struggle he faced as a young man…understanding the depths of his struggles and passion for service…has not only provided me with insight into my own story, but will do the same for many others, too.

Today's world is engulfed by crises and overwhelming need. It is full of natural and manmade disasters, extreme poverty, and preventable disease. Hot spots of suffering dominate today's headlines and tug at the strings of our hearts. Joseph is actively answering the call to do something—and to do it in a way that leaves this world a better place.

If you ever meet Joseph, it won't take you long to hear the story of the man with a bucket. It's a favorite of his—and one that shows Joseph's heart. He often tells this story of a man with a bucket of water approaching a building engulfed in flames. Near the building is a row of sleeping firemen. The man must make a choice: Does he throw his bucket on the building, or on the row of firemen?

For Joseph, the answer is simple. Wake up the firemen. Wake up the world. And ever since 1983 when Joseph founded a worldwide relief and development organization called Forward Edge International, that's exactly what he's been doing.

I have the greatest respect for Joseph and his work throughout the world. He clearly puts his "money where his mouth is" and it shows. Through Forward Edge International Joseph has mobilized thousands of volunteers to construct orphanages in Central America, provide health care to thousands in Latin America and Africa, rebuild villages in Nicaragua, repair homes in Kosovo, serve the homeless in New York City, build permanent homes for tsunami survivors in Sri Lanka, and work to rebuild communities in Mississippi, Louisiana, and Alabama following Hurricane Katrina.

Joseph has had a long-term impact on cities and nations throughout the world. He and his organization have helped tens of thousands. And Joseph will be the first to tell you—he is just getting started.

This is a powerful story of one man hearing the voice of God and doing something powerful as a result. I know you will be encouraged and challenged as you read it.

Kevin Palau
President
Luis Palau Association
December, 2009

Prologue

In the summer of 2008, I posted several job openings on craigslist. I was stunned to receive more than 300 resumes—most from the Portland, Oregon, area where our international relief and development organization is based, but some from as far away as Europe and Africa. In the weeks and months that followed, I would interview more than 25 applicants.

"Why do you want to work here?" I would ask each one at some point in the interview. The reply was always the same.

"I want to do something *meaningful* with my life," they would say in so many words. "I want to do more than make money. I need to feel like my life matters…like I'm making a difference."

The response was so consistent, so heartfelt, that I could not help but sense that I was hearing not just the longing of a handful of job seekers, but the cry of every human heart, in every place, since the beginning of time.

At some point all of us confront the question: How do I find and fulfill the central purpose of my life? We may not consciously seek an answer to this question. Other goals entice: wealth, fame, power, position, knowledge, friendships. But until our thirst for meaning is quenched such goals eventually become hollow and unfulfilling. For some the hollowness leads to what Henry Thoreau called "lives of quiet desperation"; for others the emptiness and aimlessness deepens into a stronger despair.

Closely related to this thirst for meaning is our yearning for love and approval—not just from others, but ourselves. "The basic personal need of each person is to regard himself as a worthwhile human being," psychologist and author Larry Crabb states. And the ways we seek to satisfy this need are as varied as humanity itself.

But if we are to discover our life purpose—and find the love and approval we crave—we must face the pain and brokenness in our lives. It's a decision that takes courage and honesty. Sadly, we often choose to hide behind whatever façade of "wellness" we can fashion for ourselves, whether conventional or unconventional, heroic or anti-heroic, worldly or religious. But only when we allow light to shine on the deepest, darkest secrets of our hearts can we move in the direction of wholeness and authenticity.

When I first set out to write this book, I considered writing a "how-to" book with illustrations. In the end, though, I decided to write a personal-experience narrative. Not because I thought my story was more interesting or exceptional than anyone else's, but because I believe in the power of stories. "Throughout history we have lived by stories," author Eugene Peterson affirms. "Stories draw us into worlds bigger than ourselves. They invite us to participate, to identify with the characters, to get caught up in the emotion of them. They help us to live."

I hope the story that follows will help you find, clarify, and communicate the story that is uniquely your own. And may that story be part of a larger story—one with a purpose, a mission, and a message bigger than yourself.

— *Joseph Anfuso, January 2010*
http://www.facebook.com/messageinabody

Chapter One

I REMEMBER THE LOOK ON GARY'S face the first time I invited him to join me on a trip to Nicaragua. His green eyes widened, and beads of sweat gathered on his forehead like miniature stop signs. *Nicaragua?* I could almost hear him thinking. *Why would I want to go there?*

But Gary was just the person we needed in Nicaragua, even if he didn't know it yet. The girls were fighting for their lives and deserved a decent place to live. I had a feeling Gary could help make that happen.

"Well...maybe," he had said at the time. "I'll think about it."

Several days later, I received a phone call from Gary. "I'll go with you, Joe," he said, a hint of uncertainty in his voice. "But I can't commit to anything yet. Frankly, I'm not sure how you got involved in all this, much less why *I* should get involved."

Four weeks later, I was sitting with Gary in the terminal of Houston's George Bush Intercontinental Airport. We were seated at the far end of Terminal A in a cluster of chairs near a giant wall of glass that looked out onto the tarmac.

"I almost backed out, you know," Gary confided. "When you first mentioned Nicaragua, all I could think about was Sandinistas and AK47s. I kept trying to think of reasons to cancel. But my wife finally said, 'Gary, I think you're supposed to go.'"

"You won't regret it, Gary," I said. "It's not enough to hear about the situation. You have to see it for yourself."

At last the announcement came for our flight to Managua. "Here we go," I said, reaching for my carry-on bag. "Next stop...*Nicaragua!*"

Three hours later, we were making our descent into Nicaragua's capital city. Gazing through my window at distant volcanoes hovering above Lago de Nicaragua, I reflected back on my first trip to Managua, 25 years earlier.

It was 1982, just 31 months after Daniel Ortega and the Sandinistas had wrested power from Nicaragua's notorious dictator, Anastasio Somoza. I had gone to Nicaragua to visit a missionary friend, Bob Trolese. I remember arriving at what was then a small, dingy terminal guarded inside and out by rifle-toting soldiers. "Where are you, Bob?" I remember fretting as I stood alone in the dark outside the terminal.

Now, a quarter century later, I was standing with Gary in the baggage claim area of Managua's new terminal. Still tiny compared with those of other capital cities, the terminal was dramatically different from the one I'd arrived in years earlier. It now had escalators, duty-free shops, and twenty-something tourists toting surf boards in state-of-the-art travel bags. Although the poorest country in Latin America, Nicaragua had become in recent years an increasingly popular destination for adventuresome travelers, real estate investors, and North American retirees.

On exiting the terminal, I quickly spotted Wilbert and Gloria. As always, we were glad to see each other.

"Hola, Joseph!" Wilbert shouted, lifting his arms above his crutches. A short, stocky man with smiling eyes, Wilbert had contracted polio as a boy and used crutches ever since. In spite of this—or perhaps because of it—he was one of the least disabled people I had ever known.

"Hola," I replied, wrapping my arms around Wilbert's well-muscled shoulders. "Cómo está?"

"Bien, e tú?"

"Bien, bien."

"How was your trip?" Wilbert's wife, Gloria, asked. Though shorter even than Wilbert, Gloria had a presence about her, an inner strength and authority that was immediately apparent. I had known her much longer than Wilbert, back when she was single and a field coordinator for Forward Edge, the international relief and development organization I had founded in the early 1980s.

"No problems," I said. "Just the usual layover in Houston. But at least I had someone to keep me company."

I turned toward Gary. "This is Gary Eckelman...the architect I've been telling you about."

"Hola, Gary," Gloria smiled, her brown eyes twinkling. "We've been looking forward to meeting you. Welcome to our country."

It was Gloria who had paved the way for our latest project in Nicaragua: a "village" for girls living in the Managua city dump. The fifth of nine children, Gloria had a heart as big as her country and faith that could move volcanoes. Years earlier, she had turned down a free ride at a university in the States, saying: "I want to stay in Nicaragua. My heart is with my people."

Gary and I tossed our luggage into the bed of Wilbert's pickup and slid into the backseat. Balancing himself at the driver-side door, Wilbert passed his crutches, one after the other, to Gloria, who angled them deftly between the two front seats. Soon we were speeding along the unmarked streets of Managua: the world's only capital city without street signs. Addresses in Managua were signified by landmarks, either existing or historical: *From where Sandy's used to be, 200 meters up (referring to where the sun rises), across from the big hotel.* Now and then Wilbert swerved to avoid a horse-drawn cart or a street urchin hawking cashews in small plastic bags.

At a stoplight crowded with vendors, I asked Gloria, "How are the girls?"

"They keep asking about the Village," she said. *"When will it be ready? When will it be ready?'* I'm worried about them, Joseph. If we wait much longer we're going to lose them."

My heart sank. In Managua's garbage dump—La Chureca as it was called—girls as young as nine were sold into prostitution to truck drivers who delivered the daily loads of trash. In exchange for their bodies, the girls and their families were given first access to the garbage. To ease their pain, many sniffed glue or shacked up with men three or four times their age. The longer we waited, I knew, the more likely—for some girls at least—it would be too late.

At last we arrived at Pastor Ricardo's, a two-story house—spacious by Nicaraguan standards—at the end of a narrow dirt road. It was here that hundreds of Forward Edge volunteers had lodged over the years, beneficiaries of Pastor Ricardo and his wife Leyda's extraordinary hospitality. When we arrived, Ricardo's daughter, Susan, was dribbling a basketball on a slab of concrete just outside the front door.

"Hi, Joseph," Susan shouted in perfect English, tossing me the basketball. "Want to play HORSE?"

"Hi, Susan," I smiled and gave her a hug. "Good to see you again. Maybe later, okay? Say hi to my friend, Gary."

"Hola, Gary," Susan said, extending her hand. "Have you come to Nicaragua to help Wilbert and Gloria?"

"Well…I…don't really know yet," Gary stammered. "I came to find out."

That night, Gary and I were treated to one of Leyda's famous meals: fried chicken, salad, beans and tortillas washed down with a pitcher of sweet lemonada. Ricardo was working late that night, so we decided to turn in early. Tomorrow would be a busy day.

❋❋❋

We were awakened by the cackling of a neighbor's rooster, an alarm clock I'd grown accustomed to over the years. Shortly after breakfast— eggs, toast and Nicaraguan coffee—Gloria and Wilbert arrived. The time had come for Gary to see "the situation" I'd been telling him about.

A YOUNG GIRL IN THE MANAGUA,
NICARAGUA GARBAGE DUMP.

After more than thirty years traipsing the globe, I knew that first-time visitors to the developing world could be divided into two categories: those who couldn't wait to come back, and those who would never return. *Which category would Gary fall into?* I wondered.

As Wilbert steered through the chaos of Managua's streets, Gary stared silently at the passing scenery, his eyes widening with each peculiar image: stray cows strolling calmly across the road; children pushing wooden wheelbarrows full of wood; buses and trucks crammed to overflowing with riders; and the occasional horse-drawn cart.

"How's it going, Gary?" I asked.

There was a pause.

"I...I guess I'm a little overwhelmed," he finally said. "I'm just taking it all in."

"It can be a shock at first," I said. "But you'll get used to it."

But would he? If *this* was overwhelming for Gary, what would he think of La Chureca?

Just then Wilbert turned sharply onto a nondescript street. Suddenly, the relative normalcy of Managua's main thoroughfares was replaced by a vision of hell. Here and there along the narrow, walled-in street, soot-covered men and women, many with sacks over their shoulders, shuffled like prisoners in a concentration camp. In the distance, small fires flared amid mountains of trash. Drawing near, we saw men, women and children, along with pigs, dogs and cows, sifting through the trash like flies on a carcass. A squadron of buzzards circled eerily overhead.

As Wilbert drove deeper into the dump, the scene became even more disturbing. Naked children could be seen playing outside "homes" made from odd scraps of wood and tin salvaged from the landfill. *How could anyone live like this?* I remembered thinking the first time I'd visited La Chureca. Yet nearly two thousand people lived in this hellhole—part of a marginalized community that had existed in the dump for generations.

Suddenly, Gloria tapped Wilbert on the shoulder and told him to stop. Rolling down her window, she called to a young girl who was picking through garbage on a nearby trash pile. An overpowering smell wafted into the truck like the stench of a thousand cadavers.

"Hola, Monica!" Gloria shouted to the girl. The girl turned. Recognizing Gloria, she began walking slowly toward Wilbert's truck. Strikingly beautiful despite the streaks of filth on her face, she appeared to be in her middle teens. When she reached the truck, Gloria told her something in Spanish, something I could not understand. But I could tell from Gloria's tone that they were words of loving exhortation. The girl did not respond. She just stared blankly at the ground, her face a mask of resignation.

Soon several other girls had gathered around the truck. Over the years, Gloria had befriended dozens of children at La Chureca, along with their families. She had become a kind of sunbeam to them, a ray of hope in a bleak, shadowy world that most of them would never leave.

After ten or fifteen minutes, Gloria said goodbye to the girls and Wilbert guided his truck down a narrow dirt road to a walled-in compound in the heart of the landfill.

"What did you say to that girl?" Gary asked. "The one you called Monica."

"I'm concerned for her," Gloria replied, not answering Gary's question directly. "She's been sleeping with truck drivers since she was ten. Now she's living with a man in his fifties. I thought we could save her...but now I'm not so sure."

We exited the truck and passed through a green metal gate into what appeared to be a kind of oasis in the desert of the dump: a missionary-run school attended by more than three hundred La Chureca children. The contrast between the school and landfill was startling. Unlike the dirt-floor huts of the dump, the school's classrooms were tiled, and at the far end of the compound were the landfill's only showers. Brightly-painted murals covered many of the interior walls, and the laughter of children filled the air. A recent visitor from the States had called the school "a flower growing out of a cow paddy." And he was right.

We had barely passed through the gate when Gloria was mobbed by a sea of beaming children. "Gloria! Gloria!" they screamed, their arms reaching up to hug her.

Meanwhile, I scanned the courtyard for someone else. I was beginning to think she might not have come to school that day when I saw her at the far end of the courtyard.

"Perla!" I shouted. "Hola, Perla!"

A younger version of Gloria, Perla had a pretty round face, thick black hair and deep brown eyes.

As soon as she saw me, her face lit up.

"Hola, Joseph," she cooed as I drew near. Gazing into her doe-like eyes, I was, as always, both charmed and burdened.

"Cómo está, Perla?"

"Bien," she replied shyly, her eyes glancing downward. "E tú?"

"Bien, bien," I said.

Just then, Gloria came up beside me, and, with her help, I asked Perla if she was looking forward to living at the Village.

"Si, si!" Perla said, her brown eyes sparkling. "Will it be ready soon?"

"Yes, soon, Perla…soon. Don't worry. God is with us."

At fifteen, Perla would be the oldest girl at the Village, if we could get it built. The longer we waited, though, the more vulnerable Perla became. For just as vultures feasted on La Chureca's garbage, the truckers feasted on its girls.

Gary and I would spend the next two days visiting the various locations where Forward Edge teams had served over the years: a children's home called "El Cañón"; a baby orphanage run by missionaries from South Carolina; and a government-run orphanage on the outskirts of town. By the end of day three, I could restrain myself no longer.

"So, what do you think, Gary?" I asked him as we sat together in large handmade rocking chairs on the patio at Pastor Ricardo's. "Will you design the Village for us?"

There was a long pause.

"Actually, I knew the moment I saw Monica...the girl Gloria called out to in the dump," Gary said. "She broke my heart. I've never seen such empty, hopeless eyes. Yes...I'll design the Village for you. But on one condition."

"What's that?" I asked, bracing myself.

"That you tell me how you got involved in all this. I know you came from a prominent family in New York, and that you spent years traveling around the world. But what inspired you to start an organization like Forward Edge?"

The question startled me. But it was less shocking than the five-figure fee I feared Gary might ask for his services.

"Well, it's a long story, Gary," I said. "It would take hou—"

"That's fine," Gary cut me off. "If I'm going to design the Village, we'll need to make several trips to Nicaragua. We'll have hours in the Houston airport alone!"

I was flattered by Gary's interest, but, more than anything, I sensed in Gary not just interest in my story, but a longing for a different, more meaningful story of his own.

"Are you sure?" I asked.

"It's my one condition."

The next afternoon, after catching an early-morning flight from Managua, I was sitting with Gary in the cluster of chairs at the far end of Terminal A in Houston's George Bush Airport.

"Like I said, Gary, it's a long story. But by the end, I think you'll have a pretty good idea of how I got involved in all this, and how my story relates to yours, too. A room full of pictures may be the best place to start."

"A room full of pictures?" Gary asked, a puzzled look on his face. "Did something happen to you in a museum?"

"Well, not exactly," I grinned ruefully, remembering. "It was actually the den of my family's home in New Jersey."

Chapter Two

I CLOSED MY EYES, REMEMBERING BACK forty years, remembering
a hot summer afternoon in Atlantic Highlands, New Jersey. My
twin brother, Frank, and I were sitting on the floor of our basement
den sifting through stacks of black-and-white photographs sent from
our father's newly-vacated offices in Washington, D.C. Having just
completed his fifth and final term in Congress, Dad was home relaxing
and planning his upcoming campaign for Justice of the New York State
Supreme Court. I recalled my deep feelings of awe and anxiety as I
surveyed the pictorial record of Dad's success.

"It was July, 1961," I began, "and my twin brother, Frank, and I
were home in New Jersey working on a special project for our father."
Our assignment: hang several boxes of photographs—each depicting our
father with a well-known political, religious or Hollywood personality—
on the walls of our den.

All around us were the trappings of Dad's success: a redwood sauna,
a mahogany pool table, a massive brick fireplace, and between the sauna
and fireplace, a color console TV, something of a luxury in the early
1960s. The den was also a museum for Dad's "trophies," including a
carved wooden Seal of the United States that hung above the fireplace; a
twelve-inch replica of the Statue of Liberty awarded to Dad by the AFL-
CIO; a silver pitcher engraved: "Victor Anfuso, A Leader With Vision";
and a Hebrew Bible from Israel's Ambassador to the United States
inscribed with the words: "To a great humanitarian, the Honorable
Victor L. Anfuso, as a tribute to his consistent friendship for the people
of Israel. On behalf of the people of Israel."

Outside the den, beyond the black, big-finned Cadillac in our
driveway, was our swimming pool, and beyond that, the tennis court,
enclosed by chain-link fence and bordered on two sides by dense rolling

woods. For years, our second home in Atlantic Highlands had been a welcome respite from the crush and confusion of New York City.

Sifting through the heap of photographs, I found myself marveling at the magnitude of Dad's success. Born in Sicily, Dad had immigrated to New York with his mother and four siblings at the age of nine. Over the next thirty-seven years, he had worked his way through law school, served with the OSS[1] behind enemy lines in World War II, and, in 1951, sought and gained election to the U.S. House of Representatives. His was a Horatio Alger story, and his long, imposing shadow had enveloped me from birth.

Just then, the sliding glass door of the den opened behind us with a thud. It was Dad. He'd been reading a book in his lounge chair beside the pool and was dressed only in baggy swimming trunks and leather sandals. His bare chest and Roman nose were smeared with suntan oil, and his head, bald except for two patches above each ear, was a painful-looking pink. A Cuban cigar, his trademark, was clenched tightly in his teeth.

"I thought I told you boys to hang those pictures," he snapped, pulling the cigar from his mouth and flicking a cube of ashes on the driveway. "I want them up by dinner, do you hear? You've been sitting there since breakfast and there isn't a picture up yet. *Now get them up!*"

He slid the door shut behind him and returned to the pool.

More anxious than ever, Frank and I tried to focus on the task at hand. But we had one daunting problem: we didn't know what we were doing! There were too many pictures, and we feared scarring the den's walls with a mass of holes.

---

1. The Office of Strategic Services (OSS) was a United States intelligence agency formed during World War II. It was the predecessor of the Central Intelligence Agency (CIA).

DAD AT THE PEAK OF HIS POLITICAL
CAREER, CIRCA 1955.

DAD BEING KNIGHTED BY POPE PIUS XXII
AT THE VATICAN IN ROME.

DAD WITH VICE PRESIDENT
LYNDON JOHNSON.

DAD SHAKING HANDS WITH PRESIDENT JOHN F. KENNEDY
OUTSIDE THE OVAL OFFICE. NOTE THE CIGAR IN HIS LEFT HAND.

And then we had what we thought was a brilliant idea. We would fix small screw eyes into each picture frame—two on the top, two on the bottom—then connect the frames with wire. That way we could hang *rows* of pictures, four in each, with only the wires from the topmost frames affixed to the den's crown molding. It was genius. We could hang all the pictures, and there wouldn't be a single hole!

Soon, I was twisting a screw eye into the corner of the first frame. It was a picture of Dad with the Roman Catholic Pontiff, Pius XII. I recalled the wonder I had felt years earlier after stumbling across a medal given to Dad by Pius XII in honor of his fight against communism in post-World War II Italy.

I wonder if Dad believes in God? I mused.

My thoughts now drifted back to one of my earliest childhood memories. Frank and I were walking with Dad and the rest of our family to St. Joseph's Roman Catholic Church on our way to Sunday Mass. Down passed the stoops and brownstones of our Brooklyn neighborhood we strolled, Dad stopping repeatedly to chat with passersby. As always, Frank and I stood silently with our three older siblings, Victor, Diana and Maria, close at our mother's side. We had all been thoroughly schooled on how to behave in front of Dad's constituents.

On reaching St. Joseph's the mood became reverent as well-dressed parishioners streamed through big wooden doors into the main sanctuary. Inside, lifelike statues, red, green and blue, peered from candle-lit niches along the church's side walls, and a huge wooden crucifix hovered above a shimmering white altar.

Midway through Mass, Dad stepped forward with the ushers to collect that week's offerings. Invariably, Dad worked the center aisle, stretching his long-handled basket down the length of each pew, smiling and nodding at each parishioner. Mass, I soon realized, was not a spiritual experience for Dad. It was a political happening, a time to fulfill

DAD WITH PRESIDENT HARRY TRUMAN.

DAD ON THE STEPS OF THE WHITE HOUSE WITH PRESIDENT
KENNEDY AND THE FIRST PRIME MINISTER OF ISRAEL,
DAVID BEN GURION.

his religious obligations and, most of all, to be seen.

For me, however, Mass had even fewer rewards. And as I sat each week with my family in the backmost row of St. Joseph's, I became increasingly convinced that if there was a God, he was someplace far, far away.

Frank and I now had three popes, a cardinal, and a New York monsignor hanging from the walls of our den. Before long, a third row was strung: a collection of '50s-era celebrities, including Red Buttons, Kim Novak, Gene Barry (star of the popular TV show, *Bat Masterson*) and legendary Italian film star Gina Lollabrigida. At last, we were ready to hang the most awe-inspiring photos: those of the politicians and heads of state.

Among the political luminaries were Harry Truman and Dwight Eisenhower; Irish and Italian presidents, Eamon de Valeria and Amintore Fanfani; the first prime minister of Israel, David Ben Gurion; cabinet members Robert McNamara and Dean Rusk; speakers of the House Sam Rayburn and John McCormack; and the current president and vice-president of the United States, John Kennedy and Lyndon B. Johnson.

It was these latter men, Kennedy and Johnson, who most captured my imagination. Just a few weeks earlier, in fact, I had met Lyndon Johnson at a black-tie affair in honor of my father at Manhattan's Astor Hotel. The main ballroom of the Astor was—for a boy of thirteen—truly awe-inspiring. I remembered gaping at the ballroom's chandeliers, the elegant box seats that hovered above the ballroom floor, and the double-decker dais, at the far end of the room, where Dad and the other dignitaries sat. Frank and I, along with Mom and our older sisters, sat at one of the round numbered tables—one of hundreds in the room that night—just in front of the dais. Our older brother, Vic Jr., sat with Dad on the dais.

Three memories from that night were still vivid in my mind. One was Vic Jr. reaching down from the dais to hand my mom a bouquet of red roses. Another was our family posing for pictures in front of the dais:

OUR FAMILY ON THE EVENING OF THE HOTEL
ASTOR AFFAIR. FRANK AND I ARE ON THE RIGHT.

Mom looking gorgeous in a sequined white gown accessorized with pearl earrings and a mink shawl (PETA would not exist for twenty years); my sisters, Diana and Maria, looking equally gorgeous in their long gowns; and Dad, Vic Jr., Frank and me garbed in spiffy black tuxedos.

It was the third memory, however, that impacted me most: Vice President Johnson, all six-foot-four of him, bending down to shake my hand. "You sure look smart in that tuxedo," he had said as he engulfed my tiny hand in his. "Your Dad must be real proud."

Dad...proud of me? I remembered thinking at the time.

It was not that I had no reason to believe Dad might be proud of me. Over the years, he had made several attempts to demonstrate his love for Frank and me. Only recently, in fact, he'd given us framed color photographs of himself with Pope John XXIII taken during a private audience at the Vatican. The inscription on my photo, written in Dad's hand, read: "To Joseph, My son whose character grows sturdier with the vintage of time, and of whom I shall always be proud."

I had also done all I could to earn Dad's approval. And, as I twisted a screw eye into a picture of Dad with John Kennedy, I reflected on one of my most recent attempts. Earlier that year, upon entering the eighth grade, I had joined a club at my school called the Forensics Club. Nothing as cool as using science to catch criminals, forensics was the art of formal debate or, in the case of my eighth-grade club, the art of speechmaking. Every member of our club committed to memory a famous speech, usually by a well-known politician, and then performed the speech at peer-level competitions around the city. The speech I had memorized was John Kennedy's 1960 address to the United Nations after the death of its beloved Secretary General, Dag Hammarskjold.

"Dag Hammarskjold is dead," I would recite the speech's opening line, my pubescent voice sometimes cracking. "But the United Nations *lives!*" The entire speech was choreographed—every third or fourth

THE AFFAIR IN HONOR OF MY FATHER AT THE HOTEL
ASTOR IN MANHATTAN.

sentence matched with an appropriate gesture or stride. I worked hard to hone my performance, and it was not unusual for me to take home a trophy for first or second place.

But even though Dad had never attended one of my tournaments—or even heard my speech—it did not prevent him from making a sudden and unexpected request just before Easter, 1963: "I want you to perform that speech of yours for some friends of mine in Palm Beach," he informed me. "I think they'll enjoy it."

Now this would not have been so terrifying for me were it not for that fact that Dad's "friends" were an intimidating group of politicos, including two U.S. congressmen, a judge, and the current U.S. Ambassador to Cuba, Earl E.T. Smith. I was petrified.

"Please, Dad. *Please* don't make me do it!" I protested on the day of my scheduled performance.

But he was insistent. "You're doing it, Joe," he growled. "And that's final."

The venue for my command performance was a swank Palm Beach hotel just up the beach from the ocean. Sometimes, over spring breaks, Frank and I would accompany our parents on the sleeper train from New York to Florida where Mom's parents lived. This was one of those occasions.

My recollection of the room where I was to give my speech—apart from the gathered dignitaries—included three oversized sofas, a wall of windows overlooking the ocean, and a row of potted plants. After a brief introduction, Dad asked me to step forward. Barely five-feet tall and dressed in a miniature black suit, I felt like a monkey in the Bronx Zoo.

"Dag Hammarskjold is dead," I began, my voice quivering. "But the United Nations *lives!*"

Sweat poured from my forehead and temples as I paced and gesticulated like a wind-up toy. At last, the speech was over, and I waited for my audience's response.

"Well done, son!" Ambassador Smith declared, rising to his feet to commend me. "You sounded like a junior senator from New York!" The others were equally effusive. "You've got a bright future ahead of you, Joe," one congressman remarked, patting me on the head. "Stay with it, son! Stay with it!"

Afterwards, alone in our family's hotel room, I peeled off my suit and stared pensively at the ocean below. I was mad at Dad for making me give the speech. But I was also gratified by the outcome. *I did it*, I thought. *I may never live up to Dad, but at least I can hold my own.*

A few weeks later, I received a letter on White House stationary. "I was pleased to learn of your able exposition of my address to the United Nations," the letter read. "Please accept my best wishes for continued success in your scholastic and all other endeavors." Barely legible at the bottom of the page was the signature of John Kennedy.

I knew, of course, that Dad had arranged for the letter. And while I was blessed to receive it, the gesture seemed distant and impersonal. My resentment of him remained.

Just then, the door of the den slid open behind us. It was Dad, returning to inspect our work. By now, twenty or thirty pictures were hanging against the den's walls, and we hoped for Dad's praise.

Several seconds passed as Dad stared blankly at the dangling photos, his once-lengthy cigar now a smoldering butt.

"What are you boys doing?" he finally barked, anger and disappointment glaring in his eyes. "Since when do you hang pictures like *that?*"

I shuddered. What had he expected? He'd never shown Frank or me how to hang pictures. He'd never shown us anything!

"Well, alright," he finally shrugged, glancing disgustedly at his watch. "You might as well keep going. But have them all up by dinner, do you understand? And don't leave a mess behind you either." He shook his head, reinserted his cigar, and returned to the pool.

I had no idea at the time how easy it was for fathers to disapprove of their children. Fatherless at eight, Dad was ill-equipped for parenting, and his own need for approval made him far more accomplished outside our home than in it. But—obsessed with my own chronic needs—I had no sympathy for Dad. I had only fear and resentment...feelings that fed a deepening suspicion that Dad's success might not be worth the effort required to achieve it.

But Dad was not the only one who made me feel small and deficient. As twins, Frank and I had grown accustomed over the years to people constantly comparing us. And, since I was several inches shorter than Frank and looked much younger, I soon anticipated these comparisons with a secret dread.

FRANK (R.) AND ME (L.) WITH ONE OF OUR GODPARENTS ON
THE DAY OF OUR FIRST COMMUNION.

Chapter Three

MY FIRST AWARENESS OF THE PHYSICAL difference between my twin brother, Frank, and me came at the age of seven. It was the morning of our First Communion and Frank and I were posing for pictures outside our three-story brownstone in Brooklyn. Dressed from head to toe in white, we were surrounded by chattering relatives, including aunts, uncles, siblings, and godparents. I remember gazing up at my older brother, Vic, as he tried to capture us with a Brownie camera. Suddenly, a voice rose obtrusively above the chatter.

"Hey, what happened to you, Joe? someone quipped. "Did Frank eat all the spinach or something?"

Though only seven, I was familiar enough with Popeye and the strength he derived from spinach to know this was no compliment. Looking down, I saw that my socks reached much higher on my legs than Frank's, and that my shorts dangled to just above my knees. Years later, I would come across the picture Vic took of us that day. I was barely smiling, but Frank was grinning broadly, his shoulders thrust backward, his chest protruding.

Why does Frank have to be so much taller? I remember muttering to myself as I walked with my family to St. Joseph's for the First Communion ceremony. *I could see if he was a little taller. But does he have to be* that *much taller?*

But I was not the only one with feelings of inferiority. Frank, too, suffered from the constant comparisons, chiefly because of my early success in the classroom.

"You're so smart, Joe," Mom would sometimes tell me in Frank's presence, admiring the gold stars on my report card. "Yes, you're a very smart boy." And since Frank's stars were not always gold, it wasn't long before he begrudgingly accepted the tag: "Not as Bright."

ANFUSO FAMILY CIRCA 1950. I'M SITTING TO THE RIGHT OF MY
MOM; FRANK IS ON DAD'S LAP; MARIA IS IN THE FOREGROUND;
AND VICTOR AND DIANA ARE STANDING IN THE REAR.

FRANK AND ME AS TODDLERS.

Not surprisingly, such comparisons sometimes produced serious strains in our relationship. It was not unusual, in fact, for minor disagreements to lead to blows, or for our daily playful jousting to leave one or the other of us hurt.

On one occasion, when we were nine, we were playing in the street outside our Brooklyn brownstone. I was sitting on the curb putting on a pair of roller skates when Frank suddenly grabbed me by the arm and yanked me to my feet. Although I only had on one skate, or perhaps because of it, Frank began twirling me in circles. A blur of stoops, trees and parked cars spun before my eyes. After several circles, Frank released me, and I warbled down the street on one leg, my arms flapping like the wings of a neighborhood pigeon. After a few feet, I tripped over a manhole cover and fell to the pavement.

A sharp pain jetted up my side. *Is that my arm?* I gasped, staring at the ill-shaped appendage in my lap. At the doctor's office a few blocks away, I learned that my left wrist was broken and that my arm would have to be placed in a cast. The full story of my injury was never divulged.

But I was not always the victim, of course. On another occasion, when we were twelve, Frank and I were home in Atlantic Highlands on spring break. We were riding our bikes in the driveway when I proposed a "don't-try-this-at-home" contest. Trapped with me in a kind of never-ending Olympics, Frank immediately signed on.

The contest consisted of coasting down the steep country lane that ran parallel to our property, then turning into our driveway at the bottom of the hill. With characteristic bravado, I volunteered to go first. Within seconds, I was speeding down the hill at thirty miles an hour. As I neared the bottom of the hill, something became frighteningly apparent: I could not safely enter our driveway without braking. Instinctively, I pressed on my pedals and swerved upright into the driveway—though I came just inches from a shin-high curb that separated our property from the neighbor's.

Before I could warn Frank that braking was a must, he had pushed off. I watched anxiously as he hurtled down the hill. *Brake, Frank, brake,* I remember thinking as he picked up speed. *Brake!*

But, determined to equal my performance, Frank did not brake, and as he drew near, I could tell from the deer-in-the-headlights expression on his face that he was in deep trouble. Without braking, or even trying to turn, Frank plowed head-on into the curb. I watched with horror— and, I'm ashamed to say, some amusement—as he catapulted high into the air, still firmly attached to his bike. After a slow-motion, mid-air cartwheel, he landed in a heap on our neighbor's lawn. Miraculously, the only injury he sustained was a gash on his left elbow.

But our most frequent and vivid rivalries were when we competed in one-on-one sports. Typical of such rivalries was a game of tackle football played in the winter of 1964. Being late December, the net on the tennis court had been taken down, the pool was covered with a plastic tarp, and the entire landscape, including the lawn on which we played, had turned to iron. As usual, Frank and I had padded ourselves with clothing: two pairs of long johns, three sweaters, and hooded sweatshirts tied tightly below our chins.

From the opening kickoff, the game took on a familiar pattern. Since Frank was bigger than me, I relied on my quickness to gain the upper hand. I repeatedly dodged his lunges until, after less than an hour, I was leading by three touchdowns. Brimming with confidence, I now decided to run straight at him, lowering my head and ramming him in the gut.

"You're an animal," he finally groaned. "I quit!"

I can still recall how good it felt to playfully help Frank off the field, his arm draped loosely across my shoulders. He might be bigger than me, I thought, but he would never be better…at least not in sports.

✳✳✳

Thankfully, competition was not the only byproduct of "twinhood"—
there was also our constant and often comforting companionship. As
the youngest of five children and twins, Frank and I were something of a
handful for our parents. And with Dad midway through his second term
in Congress and frequently out of town, it was decided that Frank and I
should spend the summer of 1954—from late June until late August—at a
camp in upstate New York. We were five years old.

Now don't get me wrong; Forest Lake Camp was beautiful: 180
acres in the Adirondack Mountains, complete with playing fields, log
cabins, a rifle range, and a private lake encircled by thick groves of
maple, alder and birch. It was just that at age five, Frank and I were more
interested in our mother than cabins or trees.

That first summer, in fact, was traumatic. Soon after our arrival
at Forest Lake, I took ill, and to this day I'm not sure if it was physical
or emotional. Whatever the case, I ended up spending most of that
summer in a cot in the Forest Lake infirmary. Fortunately, I was
blessed by the round-the-clock care of Nurse Doherty, a small, grey-
haired woman perpetually outfitted in a starched white uniform. I
knew nothing about angels at the time, but that summer at camp
Nurse Doherty was surely one to me.

In addition to Nurse Doherty, I was comforted by two other
blessings that summer: periodic visits from my mother and sister,
Maria, and a nightly camp ritual that brought me indescribable peace.
Every evening at Forest Lake, immediately after lights out, the sound
of a phonograph needle scratching across a vinyl record could be heard
throughout the camp from speakers not far from the infirmary. By the
end of week one, lying on my cot in the darkness of the infirmary, I
began to eagerly look forward to this sound, for after just a few seconds,

FRANK AND ME WITH OUR CABIN MATES AT FOREST LAKE
CAMP. I'M IN THE FRONT ROW, SECOND FROM THE RIGHT;
FRANK IS IN THE FRONT ROW ON THE FAR LEFT.

the scratching of the needle gave way to the most beautiful music I had ever heard.

"Our Faaather…which art in heaaaven…hallowed beeeee…Thyyy Naaame…"

Too young to fully grasp the meaning of the song, I simply allowed its smooth, reassuring cadence to caress me like a flannel sheet. For the next ten summers—all spent with Frank at Forest Lake—Perry Como's *Our Father* would be the inspirational capstone of every day.

Though that first summer had been awful, it wasn't long before summers at Forest Lake became the happiest days of our childhood. Accustomed to playing stickball in the street, Frank and I were quickly seduced by the beauty of the Adirondacks and the awesome activities at camp. It was here that we learned to swim, play sports, paddle a canoe, catch frogs, climb mountains, and gaze at the stars through a telescope. How incredible to see for the first time the craters of the moon, the clouds of Jupiter, and the rings of Saturn—objects that would have been hidden to us in the city, even through a telescope. I was intuitively aware not only of a beauty I had never seen before, but that the world was far greater than anything I could comprehend.

And while the stars and planets above Forest Lake were a distant signal to me of a world greater than I could grasp, the lake itself was a close and constant reminder. Each day we would hike along the narrow trail that led to the lake where we would spend hours swimming and diving. Now and then we would take rowboats or canoes into the heart of the lake, stopping invariably at Lookout Rock, a moss-covered boulder that seemed to grow smaller with each passing year.

But summers at Forest Lake did not last forever, and unexpected circumstances soon made the rest of the year increasingly painful. Life insisted on charging in on us, it seemed, and one circumstance in particular forced Frank and me to draw on every coping skill at our disposal.

Chapter Four

In the winter of 1960, Dad was at the peak of his political career, and since he insisted that Mom spend more time with him in Washington, Frank and I were sent off to a Roman Catholic boarding school on Long Island called Coindre Hall. We were eleven years old.

I vividly recall the day of our arrival at Coindre Hall. It was a brisk New York morning, and the grounds of the school were blanketed with snow. As we drove with Mom through the front gate, I remember seeing a flock of boys sledding down a hill just inside the school's grounds. *That looks like fun!* I remember thinking.

After a lengthy exchange of hugs and kisses, Mom left us in the care of Coindre Hall's headmaster, Vincent Paul. A tall, spectacled man in a black robe cinched at the waist by a cord, Brother Vincent turned instantaneously serious as soon as our mother left. Without a word, he led Frank and me up a long flight of stairs to a cavernous dormitory filled with rows of metal cots. *I don't know if I'm going to like this*, I remember thinking. Later that day, Frank and I were seated with approximately 60 other boys in the school's main assembly hall.

"We're pleased to have two new students with us today," Brother Vincent announced, turning in our direction. "Joe and Frank Anfuso are from Brooklyn and will be entering the second semester of the seventh grade. I hope you will join me in helping them feel at home."

From the icy stares Frank and I received, we suspected that Coindre Hall might not live up to everything the word "home" typically implied. It didn't take long for our suspicions to be proven correct. That evening, just before bedtime, Frank and I were herded with the rest of our new schoolmates into the Coindre Hall locker room. It was time for daily showers, and Brother Vincent had taken pains to inform Frank and me that these were always to be taken in silence.

Having spent six summers at Forest Lake, it was not unusual for me to disrobe in the presence of other boys. What *was* unusual, however, was the large wooden trough filled with powder that lay on the floor just outside the showers. *What's* that *for?* I wondered.

I soon found out. Mimicking the other boys, I exited the showers and stomped through the trough, taking care to cover my feet with the mysterious powder—an anti-fungal treatment, I assumed.

Back at my locker, I felt an irresistible urge to comment on the odd procedure. "Weird, huh?" I whispered to the boy next to me, nodding toward the trough.

"Anfuso!" Brother Vincent barked, shattering the silence of the locker room. "Come over here!" I looked up to see an eerie smirk on the headmaster's face. I sensed, with considerable trepidation, that he wanted to make an example of me. With my heart pounding, I shuffled passed a gauntlet of gawking boys toward my towering accuser.

"Take off your towel and touch your toes," Brother Vincent commanded.

I hesitated. It was one thing to be naked when people were going about their business; it was another when every eye was fixed on *me*.

But I had no choice. Apprehensively, I dropped my towel and bent to touch my toes. From the corner of my eye, I could see Brother Vincent reaching for a long wooden plank. *That's from a sled!* I gasped, recalling the boys I had seen earlier in the day on the hill near the Coindre Hall gate.

Before I could reach my toes, the plank smacked loudly against my buttocks. Whatever blood wasn't rushing buttward, sped to my face, and I struggled to choke back tears. Mercifully, the penalty for talking in the locker room was just one whack. Draping myself in my towel again, I retreated in utter humiliation to my locker as Frank looked on helplessly.

That night, lying alone in the darkness of the Coindre Hall dorm,

I observed a thick, new shield beginning to form around my heart. If I was going to make it in this world, I resolved, I would have to protect myself. And it wasn't long before self-protection began morphing into a kind of self-destructive daring.

An early example of this occurred that summer when Frank and I returned to camp. It was early July, right after Independence Day, and for some reason I challenged one of the Forest Lake counselors—a six-foot-four bruiser named Mitch—to swat me on my bottom as hard as he could. If I didn't cry, I proposed, my reward would be a Hershey bar, a prized commodity at Forest Lake. At first reticent, but egged on by the other campers, Mitch finally agreed.

Whack, came the sound of Mitch's palm against my tiny butt. I couldn't have weighed more than seventy pounds at the time, and the blow sent me flying. *Don't cry...don't cry*, I remember chanting to myself, tears welling up in my eyes as I struggled to my feet. Somehow I managed to keep the tears from falling, but with Mitch and the other campers scrutinizing my face, I failed to muffle a faint, barely-audible whimper.

"You cried! You cried!" the campers shouted.

For ten or fifteen seconds, Mitch gazed down at me with a mix of admiration and pity. Then he pronounced his verdict.

"I'm afraid that counts as crying, Joe," he said with some sadness. "I can't give you the Hershey bar."

Naturally, I was disappointed. *A whimper's not crying!* I protested to myself. But my sorrow was soon replaced by satisfaction. I had faced off with Goliath and lived to tell about it. Though I did not realize it at the time, seeds of grit and self-reliance—sown before I was born—were now sprouting in my heart, and their fruit would nourish me for years to come.

Chapter Five

AFTER JUST SIX MONTHS AT COINDRE Hall, Frank and I convinced our parents to transfer us to another Roman Catholic boarding school, Mount Saint Michael's Academy in the Bronx. One square block of buildings and athletic fields ringed by an ivy-covered wall, The Mount was little improvement from Coindre Hall (corporal punishment was practiced there, too), but we could at least return home on weekends. It helped, too, that Frank and I were six months older and more familiar with the rigors and regimen of boarding school life.

My first year at The Mount, still feeling pressure to follow in Dad's footsteps, I devoted myself to my studies. By the end of the eighth grade, I ranked second in my class and was a member of the student council, an honor signified by a blue and gold armband on the sleeve of my blazer. I was, as the congressman in Palm Beach had exhorted me, "staying with it."

But over the next two years, life at The Mount became a tedious blur of study halls, recreation periods and communal showers. We lived for Fridays, when we would pack our suitcases, take the subway to Port Authority Bus Terminal in Manhattan, and board a Greyhound for our intermittent "home" in Atlantic Highlands. We treasured weekends, dreading the countdown on Sunday nights, knowing that at 4:00 am the next morning we would have to dress, re-pack, and return to our captivity at The Mount. We were fortunate, at least, to have each other, and throughout that season of our lives the old adage, "Misery loves company," strongly applied.

It wasn't long, though, before the rigors of boarding school and my growing disillusionment with Dad took its toll. By the middle of my sophomore year, my grades began to plummet, and I made no effort to run for student council or participate in forensics. I still believed that I would follow in my Dad's footsteps someday and attend law school, but it wasn't anything I looked forward to.

Then, in the summer after my sophomore year, something happened that weakened still further my diminishing self image. It was the first summer in eleven years that Frank and I had not gone to camp, and we were gripped by a strong fascination with the opposite sex. Finally, after much cajoling, we convinced our mother to drop us off at a nearby dance. Having spent four years at all-male Catholic boarding schools, the dance was a frightening first step into a world of risk and mystery.

Before leaving home, Frank and I did our best to look attractive. Clearasil was dabbed meticulously on every blemish, mouthwash repeatedly gargled, and English Leather splashed liberally on each cheek. *I'm as good a catch as Frank,* I subconsciously assumed as we pulled from our driveway.

Arriving at the dance we found a small army of kids—all strangers—filling to capacity a huge gymnasium. The gym's backboards had been raised to make room for a large wooden stage where a local band cranked out a crude but exuberant version of *Gloria*, one of that summer's big hits. Surrounding us on every side—in skin-tight T-shirts, cut-off shorts, and open-toed sandals—were the most dazzling and intimidating array of girls I had ever seen in my life.

After an hour of scanning the gym and trying to think of one-liners, I finally spotted a cute brunette standing just in front of the stage. Turning to point her out to Frank, I was surprised to find that he was no longer with me. *He must have gone outside*, I thought, and headed for the nearest exit.

As the gym door closed behind me, the sound of the band faded and a sea of summer stars twinkled brightly overhead. Glancing around, I spotted Frank standing at the edge of the parking lot. To my surprise, he was not alone—he was encircled by three girls (three!), who appeared to be ogling him with rapt attention.

I froze. *What should I do?* Part of me wanted to rush right up and introduce myself; but another, more self-protective part, had second thoughts. Over the years, I had come to dread being introduced as Frank's twin. "You guys are *twins?*" people would often react. "You look like brothers…but I'd have never thought you were *twins!*" There was always something about the way their voices went up an octave when they said the word "twins" that made me cringe.

Fearful of this reaction, I retreated sheepishly into the safety of the gym. Taking risks was not uncommon for me. But at fifteen, the risk of prompt and unequivocal rejection was a peril I would do anything to avoid.

In the months and years that followed, I would resign myself to the fact that when it came to girls, I could not compete with Frank. I might not be chopped liver, but I was no match for my taller, more outgoing twin.

✳✳✳

At the start of our senior year at The Mount, Frank and I attended a weekend retreat at a Roman Catholic facility in upstate New York called Gonzaga. The purpose of the retreat was to give Mount seniors an opportunity to ask God if he might be calling them to the priesthood.

We arrived at Gonzaga, along with the rest of our classmates, late on a Friday afternoon. The main retreat house, a three-story building covered with ivy, stood amid tall oak and maple trees, red, brown and yellow with the colors of fall. On arrival, I was assigned to a small private room on the building's second floor, an arrangement refreshingly different from the sprawling cot-filled dormitories of The Mount. Plain but pleasant, the room had an old pine desk at the foot of the bed, a small crucifix on one wall, and a nightstand with several pieces of literature, all devotional, in the topmost drawer.

Throughout the weekend—during which we were not permitted to speak—we met daily in the chapel just down the hall from my room. On the final night of the retreat, the chapel was the setting for a final "pep talk" from the retreat's director, Father Stephen Thomas.

"God has a special calling on some of your lives," Father Stephen insisted, as he had repeatedly throughout the weekend. "Not much time remains before you return to your normal routines, boys. Tonight, you'll have extra time in your rooms to pray and meditate. If you haven't found peace yet about this matter, I urge you to spend time on your knees. Listen, boys…listen for God's whisper in your hearts."

That evening, I returned to my room and knelt beside my bed. I had always had a sincere if somewhat vague belief in God. And while I had no desire to become a priest, I wondered if this might be an opportunity for God to reveal himself to me in a deeper, more personal way.

"Dear God," I prayed, as earnestly as I could. "Show me your will for my life. Show me if you want me to be a priest. Show me, God. Show me."

With my forehead pressed against the mattress and my eyes shut, I waited. Ten minutes. Twenty minutes. Nothing. No stirring, no revelation, no whisper in my heart.

I decided to pray again, this time asking if God wanted me to be a brother—a calling slightly lower than that of a priest but one that still required celibacy and a lifetime of devotion.

Several more minutes passed. Still nothing. Finally, with my thoughts starting to wander, I rose to my feet and undressed. Lying alone in the darkness, I felt a strange mix of off-the-hook relief, and— there was no other word for it—rejection.

I never wanted to be a priest, I thought. *But why was there no answer to my prayers? Am I so far short of God's standards that even* he *does not approve of me?*

I now embraced what seemed at the time a reasonable and convenient perspective: I was alone in the world; and if there was a God—which I now doubted—he had no special interest in me.

THE DAY OF MY GRADUATION FROM MOUNT SAINT MICHAEL'S
ACADEMY IN THE BRONX.

Chapter Six

AFTER GRADUATING FROM HIGH SCHOOL IN 1966, Frank and I headed off to different New Jersey colleges, separated for the first time in our lives. I enrolled at Rutgers in New Brunswick; Frank at Farleigh Dickinson in Teaneck. We would not see each other again until we returned home to Atlantic Highlands for Christmas break.

It was during Christmas break, on December 28, 1966, that I was awakened in the middle of the night by car doors slamming in our driveway. Dad—now a Justice of the New York State Supreme Court—had been working in the city that week and had been due at the local bus station earlier in the evening. Someone must have driven him home, I thought. Unconcerned, I fell quickly back to sleep.

Early the next morning I heard Frank whispering something to me at the foot of my bed. I could barely make him out.

"Joe…Joe," he muttered. "It's Dad. Dad had a heart attack last night in New York. He's dead, Joe…Dad's *dead.*"

Three days later more than two thousand people gathered at a Brooklyn funeral home not far from our old neighborhood to pay my father their final respects. Dressed in a black suit and red tie, Dad was laid out in a silk-lined coffin, a thin veil of powder on his face, and a small strand of rosary beads and dwarf roses braided through his fingers. Red and white orchids filled to overflowing a dimly-lit alcove behind the coffin, as well as two large rooms adjoining the main parlor. Frank and I—just two months shy of eighteen—stood with our family on a short receiving line to the left of the coffin.

One by one the mourners filed solemnly through the receiving line. Some greeted us with pained reserve; some wept; and some reminded Frank and me of what a great man our dad had been. Among the mourners were New York City mayor, Robert Wagner; the

Archbishop of Brooklyn, Brian McIntagert; and a recent New York gubernatorial candidate and close family friend, Frank O'Connor. The sitting Speaker of the House, John McCormack, telephoned from Washington to express his condolences, speaking individually with each family member, including Frank and me.

But as I stood on the receiving line beside Frank, I was surprised and slightly embarrassed by the fact that *my* strongest emotion was not sorrow, but relief. Yes, I felt some sadness, but chiefly for our mother, who now was alone. More than anything, though, I felt liberated, as if a golden anvil had been lifted from my shoulders. For with Dad's passing, all the pressures I had felt growing up—the pressure to perform, to excel, to somehow live up to my father—had vanished. And while the implications of this new freedom were not clear to me yet, the effects of my reaction to it would play out in my life for years to come.

✳✳✳

After Dad's death, there were no immediate changes in my life. I returned to Rutgers, still clinging to the notion—nurtured since childhood—that I would follow in Dad's footsteps and practice law. That February, I pledged a fraternity, Zeta Psi, and was soon dividing my time between school work and weekend parties. As an all-male college, however, Rutgers had a reputation for academics, not parties. And on the rare occasion when I was around girls, I was something of a wallflower.

By contrast, Frank's college was coed, with a longstanding reputation as a party school. My periodic phone calls to Frank confirmed that, on the dating front at least, he was leaving me in the dust. In an effort to "share the wealth," Frank fixed me up with a

Farleigh Dickinson coed, a pretty Jewish girl from Manhattan. We long-distance dated for awhile, but nothing came of the relationship. Soon my social life consisted only of weekend beer fests and hanging out with friends at the Rutgers student union.

Yet while I was far from happy, there were at least some things to rejoice about. By now the pressures of my childhood had lifted, and the regimentation of boarding school was far behind me. Even the day-to-day pressures of matching up to Frank were gone. I was, on the outside at least, freer than ever before in my life.

But what would I do with my newfound freedom? What would replace the choking pressures and values of my childhood? In whom and in what would I believe?

At six-feet-three and bald from a childhood bout with scarlet fever, Professor Lloyd Gardner was among the most striking and popular "stars" on the Rutgers faculty. In the fall of 1967, I was enrolled in one of his classes on Twentieth Century American History.

"So why do *you* think we're in Vietnam?" Gardner blared as I sat wide-eyed directly in front of his desk. "You don't think we're there to keep the world safe for democracy, do you? Are the politicians in Washington really that righteous?"

For nearly three months, I had been inculcated by Gardner's cynical views on American history. Essentially, he believed the chief concern of U.S. policymakers was not ideology, but economics. Even World War II—generally cheered as a righteous crusade in defense of freedom—was attributed by Gardner to U.S. demands for liberal trade and free markets. America, Gardner insisted, was not the altruistic Good Guy our high school history books had led us to believe.

And who was I to argue? I was barely eighteen, and Gardner was the brightest, most learned man I had ever met. He seemed, in short, like someone who *knew. It sure makes sense to me,* I eventually concluded, old judgments of Dad still festering in my heart. *If there's anyone driven by self-interest, it's a politician. So why would a politician's policies be any different?*

Meanwhile, other courses contributed to my rapidly changing worldview. In an avant-garde literature class, I read books by William Burroughs, Samuel Beckett and John Cage, and though I didn't fully understand them, I was drawn to their confident disdain of mainstream values. Radical non-conformity, I was beginning to believe, was a valid, even admirable posture in a world with no real answers of its own.

In the spring of my sophomore year at Rutgers, I moved with two friends to a small apartment several blocks from campus. By the late 1960s, New Brunswick had become a dreary, urban eyesore, and the view from our second-floor window was a picture of despair. Directly across the street, grey shingled row houses leaned like winos against an oddly-erect Laundromat splattered with graffiti. In front of the Laundromat, lines of blank-faced commuters waited endlessly for the cross-town bus. An empty billboard with faded, old advertisements peeling from its face loomed purposelessly above their heads. It was no wonder that during the previous summer, blacks had rioted in New Brunswick, as they had in Newark, Harlem and Detroit.

One April night, about a month after moving to the apartment, I was sitting in the living room reading a newly-acquired book: *One Flew Over the Cuckoo's Nest* by Ken Kesey. My roommate, Steve McHenry, or Mac as we called him, was watching television in the other room. Like most student apartments, ours had a minimum of comforts, one being the overstuffed chair in which I sat.

Racing through the book's final chapter, I felt a myraid of dots connect inside my head as Kesey's hero, Randal McMurphy, instigated a rebellion in the asylum where he'd been unjustly confined.

"What's the matter with you guys," McMurphy barked at his fellow inmates. "You guys ain't crazy! Don't you see? It's Nurse Ratched and all them other experts who make the rules around here—they're the ones who're crazy, NOT US!"[2]

Kesey's a genius, I thought, a broad, knowing grin on my face. *This world's a nuthouse... but everybody's expected to go about their business acting like it's sane!*

Just then, Mac began to shout at me from the other room. For the past few days, we had been watching news reports on the escalating war in Vietnam. I assumed Mac was calling me to watch another dreary report from Southeast Asia. Reluctantly, I put down my book and walked inside.

"What's up?" I asked.

Mac said nothing at first, his blue eyes riveted to the tube, one hand waving at me not to speak, the other pointing at the screen.

"They shot him...they shot him. Martin Luther King...they shot him. He's dead, man. He's dead!"

The news hit me like a roundhouse punch. "My God," I gasped, gaping at the motionless body of King on a balcony in Memphis. "Who would do that?" Like millions of others, I was deeply affected by King's death. America had hit bottom, I thought. *Could it get any worse?*

But in the weeks and months that followed, it did. That June, Robert Kennedy was shot and killed in Los Angeles. And three months later, hundreds of young protestors, including Mac, were "attacked by rioting police" at the Democratic National Convention in Chicago (at least that's how I saw it at the time). America, it seemed, had gone mad.

Weary of the madness and eager to fly the coop, Mac and I decided

---

2. *One Flew Over the Cuckoo's Nest* by Ken Kesey.

to enroll in a semester abroad at the City of London College in England. Frank, too, applied for an exchange program in England. I still felt pressure to honor my family name, to measure up to society's standards, to make something of my life. But—to my surprise and great relief—I would discover in England a new, easy, and less conventional way of distinguishing myself.

Chapter Seven

AFTER A BRIEF TOUR OF THE European continent with Frank, I arrived in London and settled into a townhouse in South Kensington with Mac and several other exchange students from the States. Almost immediately, we caught wind of a music festival to be held in three days on the Isle of Wight. There, Bob Dylan was scheduled to perform his first concert in three years since breaking his neck in a motorcycle accident. Two weeks earlier, I had passed on going to Woodstock which had taken place just a short drive from our home in Atlantic Highlands. This time, I was going.

Two days later, Mac and I hitchhiked to the coastal town of Southampton where more than 500,000 young people were boarding ferries for the Isle of Wight. Once on shore, we were swept along by a sea of youthful revelers to a huge natural amphitheater just inland from the coast. There, a thick-pile carpet of humanity stretched in every direction. In the distance, behind the stage, helicopters could be seen taking off and landing, presumably with their precious cargo of musicians.

"The Beatles are backstage, ya know," I overheard a Brit in the crowd boasting. "An the Rollin' Stones."

After threading our way through the multitude, we found a spot near the top of a grassy knoll that offered a panoramic view of our surroundings. It was an awesome sight. Here and there, fluttering above the city of spectators, were flags from a dozen countries, including Germany, Sweden, Italy, France, Canada, the United States and Britain. In the distance, a bare-chested boy with the longest hair I'd ever seen meandered through the crowd with his own giant "flag" affixed to a makeshift pole. The word "ACID" was painted on the flag in big red letters. On a nearby hilltop, blue-coated Bobbies stood stone-faced and motionless.

Over the next three days, as Mac and I savored the festival's dazzling array of artists—the Jefferson Airplane, The Who, The Moody Blues and

Dylan—I felt an unexpected oneness with the crowd. Something historic is happening with my generation, I remember thinking at the time. And it's happening on a global scale.

As it turned out, the Isle of Wight festival, with its blend of music, drugs and open sexuality, would set the tone for the rest of my stay in England. It wasn't long before I was rarely attending classes and appeasing the minimal demands of my professors with periodic papers. I spent most of my time attending concerts and plays, checking out museums and artistic "happenings" and teaching myself the guitar. In a matter of days, London became a kaleidoscopic party set to the soundtrack of Led Zeppelin's eponymous debut album, The Beatles' *Abbey Road*, and the debut record of a promising American artist named James Taylor.

Sometime around Thanksgiving, I was paid an unexpected visit by Frank. He'd been spending that semester two hours north of London at a placed called Wroxton Abbey. On the morning of his visit, I was sitting on the floor of my flat playing the guitar.

"Hey, man, what's happening?" Frank blared, as he burst unannounced into my room. I was struck at once by the change in his appearance. He was bearded now, and his once-short hair cascaded atop a long wool scarf that looped eccentrically around his neck. A black double-breasted overcoat hung pendulously to his knees.

"Frank!" I gasped. "What are you doing in London?"

"I thought I'd check out the big city," he smiled, giving me a bear hug and tossing his overcoat on my bed. I detected a new, childlike openness in his eyes. It was good to see him.

"So, how's Wroxton?" I asked, sitting directly across from him on the floor.

"Great, man, great. Really a trip. We live in this twelfth-century abbey filled with tapestries and antiques. There's even a lake with big white swans in it."

For the next hour, Frank rambled on about Wroxton, telling me about the new friends he had made and the new outlook on life the solitude and camaraderie had helped him to formulate. What he didn't have to tell me was what had opened the doors of his perception.

"Wanna smoke some dope?" I finally suggested, reaching for my battered guitar case. "It's the best hash in London."

Frank nodded enthusiastically. I pulled a small packet of tin foil from the case and proceeded to roll a long European-style joint. Ironically, just twelve months earlier, Frank had lectured me on the evils of drugs. But all that was behind us now, and I was glad.

"Listen, Joe, I gotta tell you about this place I visited last week. It's in Ipswich, about a hundred kilometers from here. Have you ever heard of Summerhill?"

I was instantly intrigued. Just weeks earlier, I had read a book about Summerhill by its seventy-year-old founder, A.S. Neill. I hadn't been able to put it down.

"Sure, I know Summerhill!" I exclaimed, after taking a toke on our now-ignited joint. "It's a free school. What was it like?"

"Well, I didn't see much," Frank went on. "It wasn't an official visitor's day. But I did meet Neill. And he showed me one of the playrooms."

"And?"

"It was incredible! The kids there do whatever they want. Some kids had trashed this playroom I saw, and the only thing Neill did was tell them they couldn't use it again until they cleaned it up. I mean it was *a wreck!* But Neill said he wanted them to learn self-discipline. He wanted them to discover for themselves what was right—right for *them*. That was all that mattered to him."

Frank then pulled a dog-eared copy of Neill's book from his overcoat and handed it to me.

"Turn to page 60," he said. "Read the paragraph at the top and tell me what it makes you think of…read it out loud."

I found the page and started reading.

> The function of the child is to lead his own life, not the life his
> anxious parents think he should live, nor a life according to the purposes
> of the educator who thinks he knows best. All this interference and
> guidance by adults only produces a generation of robots.[3]

"Yeah…now I remember why I couldn't put it down," I said.

"Keep going," Frank snapped. I continued reading.

> It is civilization that is sick and unhappy, and the root of the problem
> is the unfree family. Children are deadened from the cradle days. They're
> trained to say nay to life because their young lives are one long nay.
> Don't make a noise; don't masturbate; don't lie; don't steal…There are no
> problem children, only problem parents; only a problem humanity…

Looking up, I saw Frank smiling at me, the way he always did when there was something only he and I could fully comprehend.

"I know what you're thinking," I said, memories of boarding school and Dad still fresh in my mind. "We've got a lot of unraveling to do."

Two days later, Frank returned to Wroxton, and I would not see him again for several months.

✳✳✳

Although schoolwork was the least of my worries in London, I wasn't ready just yet to jettison my youthful ambitions. I took the Law School

---

3. *Summerhill* by A.S. Neill.

Admissions Test (LSAT) in London, and sent away for applications to several American law schools. A few weeks later I learned that I'd scored well on the LSAT and, with a respectable GPA of 3.5, law school seemed imminent. It was, at least, the logical next step.

One night, near the end of my term in London, I was sitting alone in my flat listening to *Abbey Road*. Aware that deadlines for law school were fast approaching, my eyes fell furtively on a tall stack of applications at the foot of my bed.

Do I even want to be a lawyer? I now wondered. For as long as I could remember, I had been on a kind of conveyer belt toward law school—the privileged heir of a safe and respectable profession. But was that *really* what I wanted?

Nearly an hour passed as I weighed my decision. Finally, I made up my mind. I would not apply to law schools. I was tired…tired of reading about life, studying about life, thinking about life. I wanted to *live* life. And even if my future was a total blank, I was getting off the conveyer belt.

Before returning to the States, Frank and I decided to make a hurried tour of the continent. Traveling in a beat-up Volkswagen van along with Mac and some of my other exchange-student friends, we crossed the English Channel at Dover and headed for Paris. It was Christmas Eve, 1969.

After checking into an inexpensive Left Bank hotel, Frank and I separated from the others to stroll the Paris streets. A light snow was falling, and the sidewalks were carpeted with a powdery white veneer.

"Joi Noel!" a bum near our hotel chimed, poking his palm into my face. I gave him two francs, savored the twinkle in his eye, and headed with Frank in the direction of the River Seine. Across the street a policeman passed, his long blue cape fluttering in the breeze as two French schoolgirls skipped gleefully at his side. All of Paris, it seemed, was brimming with frivolity and good cheer.

At last we arrived at the river, and turning the corner saw a sight that took our breath away. There, like a giant apparition, was Notre Dame, hovering in sheer, majestic silence in the midst of the falling snow. Awestruck, we crossed the wind-swept plaza that led to the cathedral, and standing at its base, gazed long at its vast facade. I scanned the great pointed arches of its portals; the row of kings that ran in a horizontal band above the portals; the magnificent rose window, a masterpiece of pink and crimson glass looming above the kings like liquid lace; and finally, the majestic towers, much higher than I had expected, that stretched with Babel-like desire heavenward.

Drunk with wonder, I imagined Quasimodo, the hunchbacked bell ringer, crouching beside a gargoyle midway up one tower. "Sanctuary!" I fancied him yelling as he leapt from one gargoyle to another, the dark-haired gypsy girl held tightly to his side.

My illusion over, I lowered my gaze to study the mass of figures clustered inside the arch of the main portal. Dominating the figures was Jesus, sitting in grim, stoic judgment of the blessed and the damned. For eight hundred years, he had been staring down sternly from that perch. He had seen armies of mail-clad knights march home from the Crusades; heard the great bells above him toll the signal for the St. Bartholomew's Massacre, and seen the slaughter that followed; watched, as he watched tonight, droves of guilt-driven faithful come, Christmas after Christmas, century after century, for midnight Mass.

Christianity is so heavy, I thought, as Frank and I stepped beneath the stony gaze of Jesus and entered the cathedral.

The view that now materialized was astonishing. Directly in front of us, dwarfed by the vast height of the interior, was a sea of wooden chairs bordered on each side by huge cylindrical columns stretching endlessly into the distance. At the far end of the nave, jeweled rays of twilight, emerald, ruby and sapphire poured through three tiers of arched, stained-glass windows. On every side a myriad of candles flickered from giant candelabra. The effect was something miraculous, supernatural, as if the whole weighty mass were suspended from heaven itself.

For more than an hour Frank and I loitered along the aisles of the cathedral, staring at row upon row of multi-colored windows glowing in the dusk of lofty vaults—some telling stories from the Bible, others celebrating saints, still others commemorating the church's benefactors, long dead. At last, we arrived at a candle-lit niche at the back of the church and, sitting irreverently on the pavement, pondered our surroundings.

What a trip, I thought, as I scanned the great vaulted arches...the marble columns...the windows of colored glass. *All this splendor and extravagance...for what?*

What, after all, *did* it stand for? Surely not freedom; not deliverance; not peace. It suddenly seemed that everything I had yearned to flee from in my life—the demands of my father, the rules and regulations of boarding school, the dead, bankrupt values of a world gone mad—were embodied in Notre Dame. I was seated, it seemed, inside a stunning but lifeless mausoleum.

"Hey, Joe," Frank suddenly whispered. "I just realized something. This is the first Christmas we've ever been away from our family...*the first one!*"

I was silent for a moment. More than miles separated us from our family now.

"Yeah, you're right," I muttered, with an odd blend of gratefulness and nostalgia.

"Why don't we light some candles?" Frank suggested. "You know... just a way of remembering."

"Sure," I said. "Why not?"

Standing up, we walked toward a rack of votive candles that

flickered in a nearby vault. Thoughts of God were far from me as I reached for the weathered metal cup filled with matches that dangled from the rack's base.

"For the family," Frank said, stretching a long-stemmed match to the wick of an unlit candle.

"For the family," I repeated, lighting the candle next to Frank's. *And for freedom,* I thought.

Chapter Eight

IT HAD TAKEN THREE TRIPS TO Nicaragua—and several hours in Houston's international airport—to tell Gary this much of my story. By now Forward Edge had purchased land in Managua for the Village, and Gary was hard at work on a design. During our long layovers in Houston, Gary had listened carefully to my story, interrupting only to ask questions or make comments.

Now, however, he sat silently in a chair at the end of Terminal A, a troubled expression on his face. *What's bothering him?* I wondered.

"You have an interesting story, Joe," he said at last. "And I've appreciated you taking the time to share it with me. But I'm starting to wonder...well...if you didn't make choices I would have never made. I mean...I guess...I guess my life's been pretty *normal*."

"I understand, Gary," I said. "But over the years I've come to believe that we're not all that different from each other, regardless of the choices we make. On the deepest level, we all yearn for the same things—love... approval...a life with meaning and purpose. Some stick to the straight and narrow; some take roads less traveled. But we're all seeking for the same things...we just seek them in different ways."

"Yeah, I guess you're right," Gary said, his face open and curious again. "So what happened to you next?"

I returned to Rutgers from England to find the entire campus—the entire country—coming apart at the seams. With the Vietnam War still raging, America's anti-war movement was at its peak. Just days after my arrival, the Rutgers ROTC building was firebombed; and just a few days after that, more than a thousand students occupied the administration building. As a longtime opponent of the war, I volunteered to serve as a peacekeeping "marshal." Midway through the protest, news circulated that four students had been shot and killed by National Guardsmen at Kent State. I now felt, like many in my generation, irreconcilably alienated from mainstream America.

Following the protest, classes at Rutgers were canceled, and essays took the place of final exams. I received a Bachelor of Arts degree in English Literature, but did not attend the commencement ceremony. Before I knew it, my formal education was over. But my informal education had just begun.

Anxious to flee America again for Europe, I worked for several weeks as a landscaper until I'd earned enough to buy a roundtrip ticket to Germany. For the next two months, I traveled by train, boat and motorcycle across Austria, Yugoslavia, Bulgaria, Turkey, Greece, Switzerland, France, and back to Britain where I ended up again at the Isle of Wight. As I sat listening to Jimi Hendrix play *The Star Spangled Banner* (just weeks before his death), I found myself musing about the direction of my life.

Travel, I thought, *that's what I really want to do. Meet new people. See new places. Collect new experiences. It's a big world out there. And there's so much I've yet to see.*

With my childhood ambitions ditched and no long-term plans, I returned to New York and took a job at a Greenwich Village bookstore. My mother, who now lived on Long Island with my older brother, Vic, urged me to apply to law school, and even offered to pay my tuition. But I had only one, rather feeble ambition now: make enough money to get back on the road.

For the next four months, I manned the cash register at the bookstore. With its edgy location on the corner of West Eighth Street and McDougal, the store attracted a menagerie of unusual misfits. There was Otis, a fifty-something black man who walked around the city with a white rabbit on his shoulder. Almost daily, Otis showed up at the store trying to sell his latest batch of wares: pencils, playing cards, cigarettes and balloons. I often wondered where he'd gotten these things, and how he got his rabbit to sit so calmly on his shoulder, but I was too afraid of the answers to ask.

There was also Mr. Sobel, a tiny man with coke-bottle glasses and a trench coat that fell to his ankles. "This is living psycho-drama!" Sobel would announce whenever he burst into the store. He would then stand in silence for several seconds before sidling up to an unsuspecting customer. "Have you ever seen a lunatic?" he would ask. There was always a pause, and then, in a Svengali-like voice, he would say, "Look into my eeeeysss."

And there were more celebrated visitors, too. Like Abbie Hoffman, co-founder of the Yippies[4] and a member of the infamous Chicago Seven.[5] During one of Hoffman's more tumultuous visits, he removed several copies of his new bestseller, *Steal This Book*, from a display rack and distributed them—free of charge—to everyone in sight. Before leaving, he turned to me at the cash register and said, "Have a nice day!" I did nothing to stop him.

But the misfits were not always visitors. There was also my co-worker, Carl Solomon. A painfully-shy man in his late forties, Carl was the guy to whom Alan Ginsburg had dedicated his poem *Howl* …a poem that began: "I saw the best minds of my generation destroyed by madness, starving hysterical naked…" Carl had met Ginsburg at a psychiatric hospital in New York (Bellevue) where Ginsburg was visiting his mother, and where Carl was a regular. A literary savant, Carl was able to recite long passages of Shakespeare, Tolstoy and Dostoevsky verbatim.

---

4. Founded in 1968, the Youth International Party, whose members were commonly called Yippies, was an offshoot of the free speech and anti-war movements of the 1960s.

5. The Chicago Seven were defendants charged with conspiracy, inciting to riot, and other charges related to protests at the 1968 Democratic National Convention in Chicago.

By the time I met him, though, he hardly spoke, and his highest priority seemed to be keeping three pencils to the left of the cash register perfectly aligned.

With no co-workers to relate to, and business frequently slow, I was able to spend long hours perusing the bookstore's shelves. I was especially interested in poetry, psychology, cosmic consciousness, and eastern religions. I read Baudelaire's *Flowers of Evil;* Gary Snyder's *The Back Country*; R.D. Laing's *The Politics of Experience*, Aldous Huxley's *Doors of Perception*; D.T. Suzuki's *An Introduction to Zen Buddhism*; and Alan Ginsburg's *Indian Journals*, an account of his travels to India in 1964. The only books I wasn't curious about were books on Christianity. Seven years in Roman Catholic boarding schools had left me deeply disinterested in that subject.

Someone who did interest me, though, was Alan Watts. A former Episcopal minister turned Buddhist, Watts was among the foremost proponents of eastern mysticism in the West. His clear, easily-accessible writing intrigued me.

> The absolutely vital thing is that we become capable of enjoyment, of living in the present, and of the discipline this involves. Without this we have nothing to give to the cause of peace or social justice, to starving Hindus and Chinese, or even our closest friends…the immediate *now* is the goal and fulfillment of all living."[6]

By early spring, 1971, I was eager to embrace this perspective and get back on the road. One of my New York pals, Stan Turbin, had been receiving exuberant letters from an ex-girlfriend who was living on a commune in northern California called China Grade. Stan and I

---

6. *The Way of Zen* by Alan Watts.

decided to hitchhike to California to check it out.

Four days later, we arrived at a flat dusty clearing in the Santa Cruz Mountains south of San Francisco. In the center of the clearing stood a large wooden A-frame dwarfed by giant redwood trees. Within minutes we met White Bear, the commune's patriarch, a giant of a man with penetrating eyes, a snow-white beard, and a small blackboard dangling around his neck. He was oddly non-conversant as we stood with him in the shadows of the A-frame.

"He's on a voice fast," a girl with frizzy red hair and hazel eyes interjected as she stepped from the A-frame to greet us. "When he wants to say something, he writes on the blackboard."

It was Stan's ex-girlfriend, Susan, who now called herself "Sunshine." For the next several hours Sunshine took us on an unhurried tour of the land. We met Alan, a tall, strikingly handsome man with long blond hair and a perfect tan; Roga, a Merlin-like Englishman who lived in a tree house cluttered with tapestries and esoteric books; Wind, a thirty-something Canadian woman with two small children; and Misty, a free-spirited California girl with waist-length hair, a lithesome physique, and experience well beyond her years.

"Where did *you* come from?" she teased. Misty smiled when Sunshine introduced us, her eyes locked on mine. Before I knew it, I was walking with Misty through a canyon of oversized ferns to a ten-foot waterfall that tumbled into a crystal pool. Without hesitating, Misty peeled off her blouse and loin cloth and jumped into the pool.

Come on in!" she teased, splashing water in my face. "Don't be shy. This is California!"

I was captivated...not only by the characters at China Grade, but by the sheer beauty of its surroundings. I had grown up enamored by the beauty of the Adirondacks; but this was something different: majestic, immense, breathtaking.

The combination of my recent readings and the libertine atmosphere of China Grade fueled my resolve to break free from the hang-ups of my past. All my life, it seemed, I'd been strangled by expectations, limited by rules, overshadowed by standards I could not meet. But all that was behind me now. At last, I was plunging into a river of new and unpredictable happenings—a river that flowed only and interminably in the present.

"Well, there's the announcement for our flight," I told Gary, standing up and reaching for my carry-on bag. "I can tell you what happened to me in California...and all the other places I went to after that...on our return trip to Portland."

Gary and I would only spend three days in Nicaragua on this trip, so it was just four days later—back again in the Houston airport—that I resumed my story.

Chapter Nine

AFTER A MONTH AT CHINA GRADE, Stan and I returned to New York to recruit Frank and several other friends for an open-ended journey west. *We'll start our own commune!* we told ourselves. All we needed was land, a garden, and a willingness to live together in harmony. Within days, we had purchased a used Ford Econoline van, replaced the back seats with mattresses, and constructed a large wooden rack to hold our camping gear and other belongings. On a cloudless day in the summer of 1971, we pulled onto Highway 80 and headed west.

But it didn't take long for our hastily-assembled "family" to unravel. And the first rift was between Stan and me.

Smart, tall and serious, Stan had seemed genuinely interested in our dream of starting a commune. It was Stan, in fact, who first thought of the idea while we were visiting China Grade. What I didn't realize, however, was that a primary reason for Stan's interest was his deep, longstanding attraction to my current girlfriend, Deborah.

Petite, spunky and free-spirited, Deborah was the quintessential "hippie chick." I knew she and Stan had been high school sweethearts, but it had been five years since high school, and both had had numerous relationships since.

Now, though, as we crept across country in the cramped, fish-bowl quarters of the van, Deborah's open affection toward me was more than Stan could take. Jealous, angry and embarrassed, he paired off with another member of our "family," a Dutch girl named Efia. But the hurt and resentment in his eyes remained.

Simultaneously, an unforeseen breakdown occurred between Frank and his longtime girlfriend, Janet. Though they had once talked of marriage, the journey west was putting their relationship to the test. Like me, Frank was sold on buying land and starting a commune. Janet, however, was a

A PHOTO OF ME (FRONT) WITH FRANK (BACK RIGHT) AND ONE OF OUR
VAN MATES JUST PRIOR TO OUR CROSS-COUNTRY TRIP TO CALIFORNIA.

city girl—sold on restaurants, museums, and plays; and with each passing farmhouse, the light in Janet's eyes grew dimmer. Desperate, Frank spent hours in the back of the van squeezing her to his side, as if their physical closeness could reconnect their hearts. But she was lost to him now. And in the desert outside Tucson, their relationship collapsed.

We were camped that night on a lonely stretch of road between Yuma and Gila Bend. Saguaro cacti, illuminated by a full moon, encircled us like giant scarecrows as the chirping of crickets mingled with the crackling of our campfire. We had just sat down for dinner, brown rice and vegetables, when Frank and Janet leaped to their feet and wandered off alone into the desert. Minutes later, Janet returned—alone—and fled without a word into the van.

Where's Frank? I wondered. Several minutes passed.

"I better go look for him," I finally sighed, setting down my plate and starting into the desert.

"Frank!" I called, peering into the endless sea of cacti. *Where is he?*

Suddenly, I heard a rustling behind me. I turned and saw Frank, bent and alone, sitting at the base of a gangly saguaro.

"Frank!" I blurted, moving quickly toward him. "Are you alright?"

His eyes were panicked, red and unblinking. He had obviously been crying. His thick black hair, shining in the moonlight, was well below his shoulders now and his face was hidden by a snarly beard. I felt as if I was staring into a slightly-distorted mirror.

"What do you want?" he snapped, a frightening coldness in his voice.

"Are you alright?" I asked again.

He said nothing. Then, with a glare that startled me, he said, "Why would *you* care if I'm alright?"

"Look, Frank, you've got to pull yourself together. Things aren't as bad as you think. You and Janet can still..."

"It's finished!" he shouted, cutting me off. "The whole thing's finished! Janet…the commune…it's never gonna happen!"

"What d'ya mean? It can happen. Just pull yourself together, man. It's gonna happen!"

And then, with Frank's eyes boring into mine, I read his thoughts. *You don't care about me, Joe. All you care about is Deborah and your own little scene. I'm your twin brother, but you're not even here for me when I need you most.*

"Look, Frank," I finally said. "I'm sorry about you and Janet. I really am…" But I could give no more. Disgusted, Frank pushed me aside and headed back alone toward the campfire.

Now, as I stood alone amid the sea of saguaro, I wondered if all any of us really cared about was ourselves: what we wanted…what we needed…what we had a right to. Stan, like me, wanted Deborah; Frank wanted Janet; Janet wanted culture. Each of us was consumed with our own desires, each committed chiefly, if not entirely, to ourselves. I still clung to the hope that somehow, someday, I might learn to love more selflessly. But when, how, or even if this was possible, I did not know.

By the time we reached California, our dream of buying land and starting a commune had evaporated. Most of the group stayed on in California, while Frank, Deborah, and I boarded a plane for Maui.

We would spend the next six months on Maui—a relatively tourist-free island at the time—each day rolling lazily into the next. We lived on the beach, in an old pineapple plantation, and in a series of rented houses. Frank and I supported ourselves by carving whale's teeth, or scrimshaw as it was called. Frank etched nineteenth-century whaling ships; I sawed the teeth into oval pendants that I etched with Om[7] signs. We didn't earn much for our efforts, but it was enough to get by.

Finally, after half a year on Maui, Deborah and I parted from Frank

---

7. A sacred syllable used as a mantra in Hinduism and Buddhism.

and joined the crew of a privately-owned yacht that was leaving for the Mainland. After twelve days at sea, Deborah and I parted ways, too. Deborah hooked up with one of the yacht's crew, and I headed off alone. With no plans, little money, and all I owned in a knapsack, I resolved to let life take me where it would.

***

The weeks and months that followed were a hodgepodge of spontaneous adventures: a freight-train ride from California to Wyoming; brief stints on various West Coast communes; an all-night peyote rite hosted by counter-culture actor Peter Coyote on his land in Colorado. If I lingered somewhere, I paid my way by chopping wood, weeding the garden, or playing Dylan, Cat Stevens and Incredible String Band tunes on my guitar. After months of wandering, I ended up in a small secluded cabin in the Sierra Mountains of California just outside Nevada City. I was alone, and glad of it.

Set amid towering ponderosa pine and douglas fir, the cabin stood peacefully at the edge of an old mining camp called Malakoff Diggins. Once a week, I hiked the five miles to town to gather supplies: oats, rice, bread, honey, potatoes, onions, and big wooden matches for the woodstove and lanterns. I found surprising pleasure in puttering about the cabin, chopping wood for the stove and cooking simple meals. Even rolling my own cigarettes, smoked and savored without hurry, brought inexplicable joy.

How good it felt to be alone, I thought. No expectations. No competition. No strife. Relationships were too draining and, more often than not, too painful.

In addition to my daily chores, I busied myself by playing the guitar and reading used books bought for pennies at a Nevada City bookstore. One night, while reading a dog-eared copy of *The Dharma Bums* by Jack Kerouac, I came across a passage that seemed to capture how I felt at the time. The book's protagonist was living alone in a Forest Ranger Station on a mountaintop in Washington State. The passage was a snippet of his private thoughts, and a reflection of my own.

> Some folks would say I was a bum, a no-good dreamer who didn't understand the significance of this very important, very real world. But I was convinced that half America would love to do what I was doing now. All those real busy hard working men trying to get somewhere in life. I bet they'd like nothing better than to live and sleep in the woods, just to sit and do nothing in the woods, like I wasn't too ashamed to do.[8]

It was during my stay at Malakoff Diggins that I received a mysterious and unexpected postcard from Frank. He was back on the Mainland now, living in a town near Sacramento called Smartsville.

"Come at once," Frank's postcard read. "I have good and important news."

---

8. *The Dharma Bums* by Jack Kerouac, p. 110.

Chapter Ten

WEARY FROM A FULL DAY OF hitchhiking, I arrived in Smartsville just before dusk. An old mining community dating back to the Gold Rush, Smartsville had the appearance of a ghost town, consisting only of a handful of modest houses, a rundown church, and a tiny convenience store with two antique gas pumps rusting out front.

How did Frank end up here? I wondered.

I entered the store and asked the clerk if there was anyone in town named Frank. It wasn't a question I'd have asked in Manhattan, but in Smartsville, it just might get an answer.

"Try the ranch," the clerk replied, pointing over my shoulder. "It's just a little ways down the road."

Strolling in the direction the clerk indicated, I came quickly to a two-story building with a sign out front that read, "Morningstar Ranch." Not much of a *ranch,* I smirked.

Just as I was thinking this a wide-eyed man in tattered blue jeans and a flannel shirt burst through the building's front door.

"Hallelujah!" he cried, running straight at me and wrestling me to the ground. "I knew you'd come! I knew it! I knew it!"

It was Frank! I hadn't recognized him at first. When I'd seen him last, he had long hair and a bushy beard. He was clean shaven now, and his hair was at least half a foot shorter.

"I knew you'd come!" Frank repeated, lifting me off the ground and locking me in a bear hug. "The Lord has brought you! The Lord has brought you!"

I was stunned. Was it possible? Frank...*a Jesus freak?*

"It's so good to see you, Joe," Frank continued, guiding me gently toward the building's front door. "I have so much to tell you. Are you hungry? We can fix you a meal."

For the next three days, I listened as Frank and his new companions told me about their newfound faith in Jesus. They read to me from the Bible, responded to my many questions, and prayed—openly and fervently—for my "salvation."

"I know it may seem crazy, Joe," Frank conceded. "But if you'll just stick around for a while…if you'll just read the Bible for yourself. You'll see that what we're telling you is *real!*"

I also spent hours with Morningstar's "pastor," Jerry Russell, a mild-mannered man with graying hair and wire-rimmed glasses.

"How could Jesus be the only way?" I remember challenging him during one of our frequent conversations. "There are many ways to God, many paths to enlightenment. What makes you think Jesus is the only way?"

"Because he said so," Russell replied, a steely conviction in his eyes. "He said, 'I am the Way, the Truth and the Life. No man can come to the Father except through Me.' That's what *Jesus* said, Joe. And he wasn't a liar."

But it would take more than "biblical authority" to convince me. Finally, after just three days in Smartsville, I told Frank I was leaving.

"I need to find my own path to God," I explained. "A path that works for me."

Tired of debating, Frank said nothing. He just stared at me, a mix of sadness and frustration in his eyes. I was sad, too. But chiefly because Frank had found something he believed in, while I still had not. I didn't realize at the time that it would be three years before Frank and I would see each other again.

Early the next morning, I gathered my belongings and headed back on the road. I decided to return to a commune I had visited months earlier in the coastal town of Mendocino. Populated with refugees from

Haight Ashbury,[9] Table Mountain was an ideal place to continue my search for "a path of my own."

***

For the next several months I immersed myself in new and by now familiar pursuits. I participated in all-night peyote rites, adding to my repertoire of Native American chants. I learned to work with leather, making myself a pair of durable but lightweight moccasins. And, of course, I continued to read books, usually of a cosmic or metaphysical nature. Once again, I paid my way by playing on the guitar, carving scrimshaw pendants, and helping out in the garden.

One of the highlights of my time at Table Mountain was a nightly ritual that was simply called "sharing time." Each evening after dinner, the Table Mountain residents gathered in a circle on the floor of the main house. A tree branch or "talking stick" was passed clockwise around the circle, with each holder having the floor to speak. Nothing was off limits during sharing time, and whether the topic was ginseng or astrology, the state of our consciousness or the state of the compost pile, our discussions were lively, engaging and usually informative.

It was during one of these sharing times, in the spring of 1971, that someone in the circle mentioned a gathering scheduled for early summer in the Rocky Mountains of Colorado. Billed as "The Gathering of the Tribes," it was expected to draw thousands of commune dwellers, both urban and rural, from across the United States and Canada. It would be the first-ever gathering of its kind.

Five weeks later, I was headed for Colorado in one of Table

---

9. In the late 1960s, the Haight Ashbury section of San Francisco was a magnet for young, counter-culture dropouts, and ground zero for 1967's "Summer of Love."

Mountain's brightly-painted school buses. Joining me were several other Table Mountain seekers, including Jason, a wiry, outspoken New Yorker who served as our driver. After four days on the road, we arrived at the Arapaho National Forest 75 miles east of Denver. There, a small army of young people was filing onto a narrow trail that disappeared into a forest of aspen and pine. Within minutes, we had joined them.

Since we planned to spend weeks if not months in the high mountains, we packed in tepees, hatchets, cooking gear, and large sacks of grain. Up and down the trail, women in buckskin skirts and moccasins lugged babies, Indian-style, in handmade pouches on their backs. At regular intervals, makeshift lean-tos appeared where volunteer "guides" offered directions or a place to rest. Finally, after more than three hours of hiking, we arrived at a large alpine meadow bordered on one side by snow-capped mountains and on the other by a slightly inclined wood. In the center of the meadow was our final destination: Strawberry Lake.

Over the next week, more than 25,000 people assembled at Strawberry Lake. Hundreds of campsites were cleared, latrines dug, and fresh water siphoned from a myriad of nearby streams. Here and there, kitchens were set up where whole wheat bread was baked in small adobe ovens and no one was turned away. There were even "hospitals" where "doctors" prescribed everything from goldenseal for mild infections to Hindu chanting for disorders of the spirit. One health center, working out of a large canvas tent, offered one-on-one counseling, its staff, all New Yorkers, calling themselves "The Woodstock Angels."

I would spend five weeks at Strawberry Lake, playing music at various campsites, cleansing myself in communal sweat lodges, and swimming in the lake. "It was the only decent activity left in the world," Jack Kerouac had declared in *The Dharma Bums*. "To be in some riverbottom somewhere...or in mountains, or in some hut in Mexico or shack in Adirondack, to rest and be kind, and do nothing else but practice what the Chinese call 'do-nothing.'"

But as the days and weeks passed, and the novelty of our gathering faded, a palpable discontent began to permeate our mountain hideaway. Finally, the gathering disbanded, and—like every place before it—Strawberry Lake simply became another place to leave.

Disappointed but still hopeful, my friends and I re-boarded our school bus and headed back toward California. In the middle of our third day on the road, somewhere outside Sacramento, Jason decided to take a detour to pick some fruit. Winding through perfectly-manicured streets, we came at last to a giant peach orchard and exited the bus. Twenty minutes later, after filling five cardboard boxes with fruit, we piled back onto the bus and began to pull away.

"Who's that?" Jason suddenly barked, pointing to the right side of the bus. I turned and saw a man with wire-rimmed glasses behind the wheel of a pickup waving for us to pull over. Uh oh, I thought. He must be a security guard. As the vehicle drew closer, though, I was startled to see that I recognized the man.

Oh, crap! I exclaimed inwardly. *It's the preacher from Smartsville... what's his name...Russell? Yeah...Jerry Russell. What's he doing here?*

I was dumbfounded. We had just driven hundreds of miles across a vast expanse of the United States and somehow managed to cross paths with my twin brother's pastor! It was uncanny.

I quickly hid myself in the back of the bus. The last thing I wanted was for Jason and my Table Mountain pals to think Russell and I were friends.

Seconds later, Russell was standing at the door of our bus with a big black bible in his hand.

"Howdy!" he drawled, a kindly grin on his face. "Can I be of some service to you folks? You looked like you might be lost."

"Lost? No, we're not lost," Jason said. "Just pickin' peaches."

"Oh, I see," Russell chirped, stepping closer. "Say...you folks wouldn't be from the Lighthouse Ranch by any chance would you?"

"Lighthouse Ranch? What's that?" Jason asked, a tinge of sarcasm in his voice.

"It's a Christian commune. Up in Eureka."

"Never heard of it," Jason snapped, reaching for the lever to shut the bus's door. "Thanks for your concern, though. We gotta be..."

"Hold on a minute," Russell interrupted, stepping even closer. And then, with the sincerity of a choirboy, he asked: "Do you folks know Jesus?"

By now my forehead was flat against my knees.

"Listen, brother, we know where you're comin' from," Jason said. "You don't have to preach to us. If you're into Jesus, that's cool. We're into him, too. We just don't have all our eggs in one basket, y'know what I mean?"

"Sure," Russell said, "I understand. But let me just tell you folks, and then I'll be goin'. Jesus *loves* you. Each one of you. And if you put your trust in him, he'll set you free."

"Well, we appreciate that," Jason snickered. "Nice talkin' with you."

"Yes. Nice talking with you," Russell smiled. "God bless you now."

"Yeah, God bless you, too."

I lifted my head just in time to see the preacher walk back slowly to his pickup and drive away.

That was close, I sighed, sitting upright again in my seat. *Can you believe that? What are the odds of bumping into my brother's pastor while driving between Denver and the Pacific Ocean?* It was too weird.

Later that evening I was back again at Table Mountain. I now had one objective, and one objective only: Find a spiritual path that would equal if not eclipse the spiritual path chosen by Frank. Not that I wanted merely to "outdo Frank," but to verify my conviction that Jesus was not the *only* way to God.

"You should go to India," one of my Table Mountain pals suggested two days after my return from Colorado. He had been to India in the late 1960s, and his fanciful descriptions fueled my imagination. "It's unlike any place on earth," he insisted. "Gurus...elephants...magic...the Himalayas...*you have to see it for yourself!*"

His suggestion fell on ready ears. Ever since childhood—when I had watched *Sabu the Elephant Boy* on television—I had been fascinated by the East. Now, after years of studying eastern religions, the prospect of going to their source opened before me like a divinely-lit trail.

For the next two weeks I devoted myself to preparing for my journey. I visited the Mendocino library and studied the route from Istanbul to New Delhi. I sewed patches on my jeans and repaired my sleeping bag. I even made plans to pick apples in Massachusetts to earn money for the trip. I wouldn't need much, I thought; just enough to buy a one-way plane ticket to Frankfurt and passage from there aboard trains, boats and buses to India.

Everything seemed to be falling into place when, on the eve of my departure for Massachusetts, Table Mountain received an unexpected guest. Sabine Ball, a fifty-something German woman and founder of a nearby commune, had been asking to visit Table Mountain for weeks. *What does she want?* we all wondered.

That evening, in keeping with our "sharing time" tradition, we gathered in a circle on the floor of the main house. Light from several lanterns danced around the room, casting shadows on the faces of those present. Sabine's face, with its piercing blue eyes, high cheekbones and peaceful smile, had a regalness about it, a quality enhanced by her long, beautifully-embroidered dress. Eager to hear what she had to say, we handed Sabine the talking stick first.

"Thank you for this opportunity," she began, a faint German accent coming through. "I know some of you know parts of my story. But what I've come to share with you tonight is so important I need to give you an even more complete and honest picture."

For the next sixty minutes, Sabine recounted the story of her remarkable life. She shared about her childhood in Nazi Germany as the daughter of a prominent doctor. She told of her escape from Germany, her teenage years in Paris, her marriage to a Miami millionaire, and their painful divorce. She explained her move from Florida to California in 1967, and her decision to buy land in Mendocino to build a haven for dropouts from the Haight. And finally, she cited her pilgrimage to India and Nepal in the spring of 1968.

"I have spent many years searching for spiritual answers," Sabine concluded. "Now, after all my years of seeking, the truth has found me."

There was a long, uncomfortable silence as everyone leaned forward to hear what Sabine would say next.

"Several weeks ago," she continued, "I was visited by members of a commune in Eureka called the Lighthouse Ranch. They spent four days with me, telling me their stories, answering my questions, and sharing with me from the Bible. Before they left, they prayed with me, and I surrendered my life to Jesus Christ. I'm a follower of Jesus now," she concluded. "And I've come here tonight to urge you to consider the claims of Christ."

No sooner had Sabine said this than she found herself in hostile territory. The "sharing time," normally a bastion of open-minded tolerance, suddenly became a shooting gallery, with Sabine in everyone's sites. Sensing she'd lost the room, Sabine passed the talking stick warily to the woman on her left.

"We're all like snowflakes," the woman said. "We must each find our own way to God."

"We have no quarrel with Jesus," Jason snapped when the stick came to him. "But if you're trying to tell us he was the *only* fully-realized being who ever lived...well, that's just ridiculous!"

"All roads lead to the same place," I said when it was my turn. "Which road we take doesn't matter, as long as we're somewhere along the way."

As soon as the final person had spoken, Sabine rose politely to her feet and said her goodbyes. In just one night, a woman once revered as a wise and thoughtful seeker had been reduced—in our minds at least—to a spiritual novice.

By noon the next day I was sticking out my thumb on the outskirts of Mendocino and heading east. I was going to India, and no one and nothing could get in my way.

Chapter Eleven

MY DECISION TO GO TO INDIA, I told Gary, was fueled by three primary impulses: 1) my thirst for adventure; 2) my longstanding interest in eastern religions; and 3) my lifelong yearning for uniqueness. All my life, it had seemed to me at least, I had languished in the shadow of someone else. First Dad, who had towered above me like a frightening colossus. Then Frank, with whom I had always, and not often favorably, been compared. But now *I* was in the driver's seat. And I was determined to build from my experiences a new, more distinctive identity. If nothing else, my journey east would add new flecks of color to my increasingly original self-portrait.

After a season picking apples in Massachusetts, I had saved enough money to buy a one-way plane ticket to Germany. From there, I would travel overland to India, a journey that I expected to take four or five weeks. My only companions, I knew, would be other western travelers I might meet along the way. The self-reliance I had cultivated since childhood would have to serve me in good stead.

On the eve of my departure, I was organizing my gear on the floor of my sister Maria's home on Long Island. I didn't have much: a sleeping bag, a multi-colored Mexican blanket, a single-burner Optimus stove, small bags of brown rice and trail mix, and maps of the Middle East and India. As I stuffed each item into my backpack, Maria and her husband, George, watched curiously from a nearby sofa.

"*Where* are you going again?" George asked for the second time since my arrival the day before. A Panasonic sales representative in his late twenties, George was anything but a navel gazer. We first met when I was seventeen, and he and Maria were seniors in college. We had always liked each other, and there was no judgment between us.

"India," I repeated, matter-of-factly.

A PHOTO OF ME TAKEN IN MANHATTAN JUST BEFORE
MY DEPARTURE FOR INDIA.

There was a long pause.

"And how much money do you have?" Maria asked, her voice heavy with concern.

"About three hundred dollars," I said.

There was another long pause.

"And *why* are you going to India?" George persisted.

I didn't answer him at first. I knew there was nothing I could say that would make sense to him.

"If I tried to explain, George, you wouldn't understand. It's just something I have to do. Don't worry. I'll be fine."

Five days later—and years before cell phones, satellite dishes or the worldwide web—I was sailing aboard a Turkish freighter eastward across the Black Sea. A cargo ship, the freighter had only one compartment for paying passengers, a small, dormitory-style room jammed with bunk beds. I would spend that night—my only night on board—sleeping on deck under the stars.

Heaven watch over me, I thought, staring at the mythological hunter, Orion. *I'm in your keep.*

It did not occur to me at the time that whatever angst and loneliness I felt—and I did feel some—were largely a result of my own choices. What little contact I had with my mom during this period had taken the form of brief, just-passing-through visits, occasional phone calls or cursorily-written postcards. The fact that she was praying for me mattered little in my opinion at the time, though I would later realize that her prayers had more to do with whatever protection I experienced than the stars overhead.

Early the next morning, I disembarked in Trabzon, a small Turkish city two hundred miles west of the Iranian border. Westerners were still something of a rarity in Trabzon, and my presence there created an instantaneous stir.

"Hey, tooreste!" children jeered, amusing themselves with wild mockery of my appearance and by tossing the occasional stone. I quickly adapted, though, hardening myself to their jeers and pretending that I belonged in this menacing place.

For the next three days, I traveled on a succession of peasant-filled buses across the most primitive terrain I had ever seen in my life: a bleak, flat expanse interrupted only by the occasional village or army post. It was not until Herat, a small town on the western edge of Afghanistan, that the overland trail suddenly became enchanted.

Although it was Afghanistan's third largest city and the most substantial community for a thousand square miles, Herat was nothing but one main street intersected by four or five unpaved roads. At first it appeared to be a poor place, like the villages of eastern Turkey, but it quickly became a kind of paradise, a haven of fruit trees, spice shops, water and shade. In the marketplace, turbaned merchants hawked their wares: silk merchants, carpet merchants, silver merchants, rope merchants, and vendors of precious and semi-precious stones. In the skin shops, I saw bear skins, leopard skins, lynx hats, and fox throat rugs. Everywhere, women in long black robes and fretwork visors squatted in the dirt to haggle prices, signaling their bids with dark, weathered fingers. Intermittently, horse-drawn carriages with brass mudguards and velvet canopies pranced through the choke of pedestrians as barefoot water boys dampened the streets with big wooden spoons. It was a scene from *Ali Baba and the Forty Thieves*, a childhood fable come to life.

Adding to the allure of Herat, for many Westerners at least, was its seemingly endless supply of drugs. Unlike Turkey or Iran, where drug offenders were routinely and severely punished, absolutely no one in Herat bothered to enforce the drug laws. Hashish was everywhere— in the shops, streets, restaurants—and while the average Afghan regarded the drug with indifference, the average Westerner consumed it voraciously, smoking it in long, funnel-shaped pipes called *chillums*. Not surprisingly, for some overland travelers, passing through Herat was a lingering transition typically experienced in one of the small, dilapidated hostels at the edge of town.

It was in one of these hostels, soon after my arrival, that I met an unlikely Western traveler who would alter the trajectory of my journey. Having arranged for a room in one of the hostels popular with Westerners, I was seated at a crude wooden table in the center of the hostel courtyard. All around me road-weary travelers sipped tea or puffed compulsively on the ever-burning chillums. The sweet smell of hash hung heavy in the air.

"Excuse me," a high-pitched voice suddenly interrupted my solitude. "Is anyone sitting here?"

I looked up and saw a petite Western woman with big brown eyes and a radiant smile standing at the edge of my table. A black embroidered shawl was draped across her shoulders, and her silver earrings glimmered in the candlelight from surrounding tables.

"May I join you?" the woman asked, before I could answer her first question. Her accent sounded French.

"Ah...sure," I stuttered, gesturing at the empty chair to my right. "Have a seat."

From the rambling conversation that followed, I learned that my new friend was a French Canadian artist from Quebec named Lizzie Tournier. She was traveling to India in a chauffeured van that she and two Québécois—gay lovers—had contracted from London to New Delhi. Little interested in eastern religion, Lizzie's passage to India was, in her words, "this year's winter vacation."

"Where in India are you going?" I asked.

"It's a place called Puri, south of Calcutta on the Bay of Bengal. The beaches are supposed to be beautiful there. And there are hardly any tourists…that's what I've been told at least."

Puri. I made a mental note of it.

"And where are *you* going?" Lizzie asked.

"I'm not sure. I don't have a plan."

We sat in silence for several seconds.

"Then why don't you join us?" she said, her brown eyes twinkling. "There's plenty of room in the van. We'll take you as far as New Delhi, and you can decide where to go from there."

I hesitated for a moment, then bobbled my head from side to side— the local gesture for "yes."

For the next three days I traveled with Lizzie and her friends across Afghanistan toward the Pakistan border. About fifty miles from the border, our van entered a kind of no-man's land, a hostile tribal zone teeming with bandits. Now and then, small bands of herdsmen appeared grouped menacingly by the side of the road. Stern, bearded men in turbans cradled ancient-looking rifles as threadbare children pelted us with stones. We did not stop to scold them.

Soon we were twisting through the Khyber Pass, a narrow, treeless canyon walled by precipitous cliffs. I remembered reading somewhere that Alexander the Great had marched his armies through the Khyber Pass on his way to the plains of India. It was a fitting portal, I thought, to the mystery and adventure that lay ahead.

Once in Pakistan, we proceeded with haste toward the Indian border. As planned, we arrived on a Thursday, the only day Westerners were permitted to cross. In a large dusty quadrangle outside the Indian customs building, a weeks' worth of overland travelers clustered beneath leafy banyan trees. We braced ourselves for a long, indeterminate wait.

Two or three hours passed when suddenly, in the midst of the quadrangle, an unexpected commotion occurred. Stepping from the van I noticed three neatly-dressed Westerners distributing leaflets to the overland travelers. Stepping closer, I bent down to pick up one of the discarded tracts. On its cover was a crude drawing of Jesus and the words: "This Was Your Life."

Jesus freaks...*here?*

Flipping through the tract, which featured sari-clad women and pictures of Nehru on the walls, I came to another drawing of Jesus seated on a giant throne above a vast sea of humanity. The caption read: "For there is one God and one mediator between God and men, the man Christ Jesus."

Oh, please, I groaned inwardly, eyeing the disruptive zealots. *Why do they always think they have a corner on truth?*

I returned the tract to the ground, then picked it up again, thinking I might one day share it with Frank who might find an Indianized version of a Christian tract amusing. *How far do I have to go to get away from proselytizing Christians?* I muttered to myself as I shoved the tract into my pocket.

Two days later—and five weeks after my arrival in Germany—our soot-covered van entered the Indian capital of New Delhi. I had made it. *And I still had two hundred dollars in my pocket!* Given the strength of the dollar in that part of the world—and my willingness to travel fifth class—I was confident I could get by in India for at least three months. My one concern: *Where do I go from New Delhi?*

"The only place I want to see in India besides Puri is the Taj Mahal," Lizzie had confided to me while we waited in the van at the India/Pakistan border. "You can join me if you like."

I had declined Lizzie's offer at the time. I had journeyed east to find "spiritual answers," and entangling myself with a woman would surely take me off course. But I was now reconsidering. What harm could there be in a one-day excursion? Agra (where the Taj Mahal was located) was just a short train ride from New Delhi. I could join Lizzie there for the day, then focus again on my spiritual quest. That night over dinner, I told her I'd changed my mind and would accompany her to the Taj.

"Wonderful!" she squealed. "I was hoping you might do that."

Our first order of business was to trade our Western garb for outfits more suited to India. Lizzie bought a sari, and I replaced my blue jeans and moccasins with baggy linen pants and rubber sandals. On the afternoon of our third day in India, we boarded the Taj Express for the two-hour train ride to Agra.

We arrived just after sunset. A full moon was rising, and the city was bathed in light. After a rickshaw ride from the train station, we came at last to the Taj entrance. Our first glimpse of the iconic building took our breath away. It would have been stunning under any circumstances, but under a full moon it was magical. Now and then, as the moon disappeared behind passing clouds, the building's marble dome shrunk back into the shadows. Then, when the cloud cover passed, it swelled to life again, as if lit from within.

Lizzie and I were mesmerized. For what must have been an hour, we sat silently on a marble bench in the Taj's perfectly-symmetrical garden.

Lizzie was the first to speak.

"It was built for love, you know," she said, her eyes fixed on the masterpiece that loomed above our heads.

"Yes, I know," I said. "By a grieving widower…it was a tomb for his wife."

We sat silently for several more seconds.

Then, Lizzie turned toward me and asked an unexpected question.

"Have you ever loved a woman, Joseph?"

I could feel the blood rushing to my face. I had had my share of relationships in recent years, always fleeting encounters centered chiefly around sex. I dreamed, of course, of meeting that "special someone." But, at twenty two, it was not my highest priority.

"I guess it depends on what you mean by love," I said.

"I used to believe in love," Lizzie sighed. "I mean…love that lasts a lifetime. In my twenties I lived with a man in Paris for two years. He was much older than me, a well-known artist, a man with real talent. I loved him. But he broke my heart. I learned not to expect too much after that.

"There's an Edith Piaf song that says what I feel about love," Lizzie continued. "Would you like to hear it?"

I bobbled my head.

Lizzie lifted her eyes toward the moon and, in a sad, barely audible voice, began to sing.

> When all seems lost, life begins again;
> There'll be another dawn tomorrow.
> After one love, another begins.
> Some guy will come whistling along
> His arms filled with spring…Tomorrow.
> The bells will ring in your sky
> You'll see a lover's moon,
> You'll smile again, love again, suffer again,
> Over and over,
> There'll be another dawn…Tomorrow.[10]

Lizzie turned to face me again. "You can spend the winter with me in Puri if you like, Joseph. We could have a nice time together."

I was stunned. I knew Lizzie liked me, and I liked her. But if I accepted her offer what would become of my spiritual quest? Had I come all the way to India just to hook up with a woman?

---

10. *Tomorrow (It Will Be Day)* by Edith Piaf.

"I'm flattered, Lizzie," I said, staring at the dome of the Taj in a nearby reflecting pond. "But there are some things I need to do first. Maybe, after a while…maybe then I'll join you."

"I hope so," Lizzie said, kissing me on the cheek. "But there's no hurry."

That night, as I lay clothed beside Lizzie in an Agra hotel room, I resolved to keep my quest for spiritual answers—for a path I could call my own—as my top priority.

The next day, Lizzie and I returned to New Delhi where she booked a flight to Calcutta, and I boarded a train for Brindavan, the sacred town where the Hindu god Krishna was born, and home of the fabled Indian guru, Neem Karoli Baba. I had come to the East to find truth, I told myself. To prove to Frank—and to myself—that there were more ways to God than Jesus Christ.

But in the days and weeks that followed, Lizzie was never far from my mind.

Chapter Twelve

I ARRIVED IN BRINDAVAN AND BOOKED a room at a boarding house popular with Neem Karoli Baba's followers. I had first heard of Neem Karoli in a book by Richard Alpert called *Be Here Now.* A colleague of Timothy Leary's at Harvard, Alpert—who now went by the name Baba Ram Dass—had met the then-obscure guru on a trip to India in 1967. In his book, Ram Dass referred to him simply as "the man with a blanket."

At the Brindavan boarding house I was disappointed to learn that Neem Karoli was seeing no one at the moment, having sequestered himself in a fenced-in ashram on the outskirts of town. With no way of knowing when I might meet the guru, I decided to explore the Brindavan streets.

Within minutes I came upon a trio of cows, dazzling white, with red-lacquered horns and garlands of marigolds, yellow and orange, dangling about their necks. Trailing the cows were saried women, their smooth brown skin set off by silver nose rings, necklaces, earrings and bracelets that tinkled when they walked. Now and then a cow would lift her tail, and before the dung had hit the ground the girls had cupped their hands and caught it, put it in their baskets, and sped away.

At first, I had been shocked by such sights. The poverty, the stench, the hopeless hordes of India had been so beyond my expectations that there was no armor possible. By now, though, after just six days in India, an icy shield had begun to form around my heart, though there were times when I wanted to cry.

Finally, I arrived at the Brindavan marketplace, a narrow, bustling street of cave-like shops and frowning merchants. After browsing for a time, I noticed a row of squatting women selling marigold garlands, just like the ones I'd seen on the cows. Touched by the sadness in their eyes,

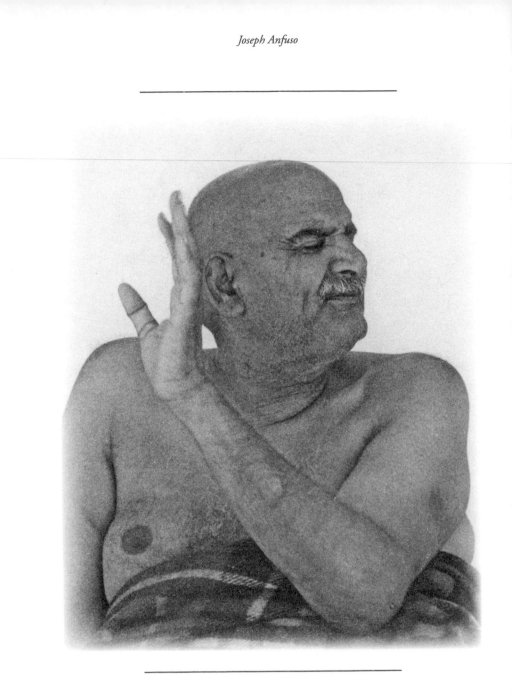

NEEM KAROLI BABA,
AKA "THE MAN WITH A BLANKET."

I bought one, and draped it around my neck.

I was continuing through the marketplace when suddenly a young girl threw herself at my feet, touched the fingers of her right hand to my toes, then touched them to her forehead several times in rapid succession. I was flabbergasted. *It must be a gesture of respect,* I thought, deeply embarrassed.

As I turned to watch the girl scurry away, I saw my reflection in a nearby window. Staring back at me was what appeared to be an eastern holy man, his long matted hair and bushy beard framed by the sun-like colors of a garland.

I chuckled. I'm no holy man, I smiled. But I sure *look* like one.

I continued on for a few more yards when I was suddenly approached by an old man with hunched shoulders and a long gray beard. The man stared at me for several seconds. Then, with a single cat-like motion, he ripped the garland from my neck, threw it on the ground, and stormed away.

I didn't know whether to laugh or cry. *I guess he didn't buy my sage-like persona,* I surmised.

Eager to leave the marketplace now, I scurried down ancient, cobbled streets to the river on the far side of town. It was unlike any river I had ever seen. Here and there along its banks, starving dogs and black-haired pigs poked hungrily for food. Here, too, were the saried dung collectors, patting their harvest of poop into pancakes which they laid in rows on rocks in the sun to dry.

So that's what they do with it, I marveled. I later learned that dried cow dung served as fuel for millions of India's poor.

I was taking all this in when I felt a tapping on my shoulder. I turned to find myself face to face with a *real* eastern holy man—a long-haired sadhu whose only possessions appeared to be a loin cloth and a small brass begging bowl.

Holding me in his gaze, the sadhu plunged into a stream of Hindi and pidgin English, fervently insisting that he and I were one (ek) and that God (Bhagavan) was everywhere in the squalor that surrounded us.

"Bhagavan ek! Bhagavan ek!" he crowed, his thin brown digit finger pointing upward. "You...sadhu...Jesus ...*ek...ek!*"

"Yes...yes," I muttered, familiar with the eastern concept of oneness—that all existence was an expression of the divine. "Yes. Bhagavan is one," I said. "You...me ...Jesus...*ek...ek.*"

At first the sadhu seemed dubious of my reply. Then he nodded in that odd Indian fashion—his head tracing the movements of a smile— muttered the Hindi word for good (acha), and walked away.

I breathed a sigh of relief. But as I turned to face the river again, I wondered if what I had just agreed to was really true. Were the pigs, dogs and dung patties—the sadhu and I—really one? Perhaps if I stayed long enough in India, it would make more sense to me.

For the next three days I waited with the rest of Neem Karoli's disciples for word of his availability. But the news was not good. "The man with a blanket is sick," I was told. It would be days if not weeks before I could see him.

I couldn't wait that long. I was tired of roaming the streets, and there was too much of India I had yet to see. Disappointed but determined, I purchased a third-class train ticket for Benares, another sacred city five hundred miles to the east.

✳✳✳

By the time the train for Benares arrived at the Brindavan station, it was already packed to overflowing. Even the luggage racks were jammed with riders perched shoulder-to-shoulder, their knees up around their ears. I entered one of the jam-packed cars and, with no reserved seat, found a space on the floor in front of the WC.

For the next ten hours, I lay in the fetal position in front of the toilet, a final obstacle for passengers needing to relieve themselves. As the train approached each station, hundreds of waiting travelers could be heard on the platform ahead, long before they could be seen. It was unnerving, especially since every square inch of my car was already occupied!

Finally, at what must have been two in the morning, I decided to abandon my post at the toilet to see if I could find a more habitable car. Jumping from the train, I ran feverishly along the platform, peering anxiously into every window. I came at last to a car that looked, to my utter amazement, almost empty. *Was it possible?* In no mood to ask questions, I quickly re-boarded the train.

I could barely believe my eyes. The car was so spacious that many of its occupants were lying across multiple seats, their bodies shrouded by blankets. Ecstatic, I grabbed a seat near the entrance, directly across from a sullen-looking man who appeared to be in his mid-thirties. I nodded to the man, but he did not respond. Too excited to sleep, I buried my nose in a copy of Herman Hesse's *Siddhartha*.

After reading for several minutes I noticed that the sullen-looking man was staring at me.

What's his problem? I wondered.

I was just about to say something when the man began screaming at me, something in Hindi, something I could not understand.

Instantly, the reclining passengers yanked back their blankets to reveal smart-looking uniforms with epaulets and shiny brass buttons. *I was traveling in a car filled with soldiers!* Before I could grasp what was happening, a soldier with a handle-bar mustache and bloodshot eyes appeared just inches from my face. He looked like an officer.

"This man says you are thief," the soldier barked, his eyes locked on mine. "He says you are thief!"

Was this really happening?

I had to defend myself, and fast.

"Me no thief," I said, with all the authority I could muster. "I am good man. No thief. *Good man. Good man.*"

The soldier stared at me for several seconds. He then twisted his mustache once or twice, glanced at my accuser, and returned to wherever he'd come from. Satisfied the problem was over, the other soldiers hid again beneath their blankets, and the car was just as I had found it. Without hesitating, I reached for my backpack and grabbed a seat as far from my accuser as I could get.

In the long dark hours that followed, I was pummeled by self-doubt. Why were these things happening to me? *Was* I "a good man"? And if I was, why had that man in Brindavan ripped the flowers from my neck? And why, of all things, would a stranger accuse me of being a thief? *Was there something about me that provoked such scornful reactions?*

Peering into the shadows of the passing landscape, I felt certain of only one thing: I was still a man in search of himself. I could only hope that somehow, someday, I might become someone that I—and others— could believe in.

At last, on December 23, 1972, I arrived in Benares—the world's oldest living city. To Hindus, Benares was the center of the universe, the most sacred spot on earth. Each year, thousands were cremated in Benares, their ashes scattered in the River Ganges. From the brightly-painted houseboat I rented on the banks of the river, ocher-red cremation pyres could be seen day and night, consuming the dead, as they had for centuries without interruption.

It was here in Benares, minutes before midnight on Christmas Eve, when I had a strange, almost dream-like experience. Unable to sleep,

I climbed the ghat[11] that led from my houseboat to the main Benares bazaar. Nearing the top, my eyes were drawn to a small cow-dung fire flickering in the shadows to my right. Peering closer, I saw huddled around the fire a band of ragged lepers. Fascinated, I paused to study the lepers as they passed a tiny chillum slowly around their circle. *How sad,* I thought.

I was about to turn away when, as if from nowhere, the words of the Brindavan sadhu echoed in the back of my mind: "Bhagavan ek… Bhagavan ek…you…me…Jesus…ek…ek." And then I thought of Christmas, just minutes away, and the shepherds of Bethlehem huddling around their fires on that first Christmas night.

Why not?

Before I could change my mind, I approached the band of lepers and squatted down to join them. Unaccustomed to such advances, they seemed suspicious of me at first. But sensing my sincerity, the leper to my right—his fingers nothing now but stumps—stretched the chillum in my direction.

Bhagavan ek…Bhagavan ek, the sadhu's words echoed in my head as I cupped the grimy chillum and placed it to my mouth. I took a puff, then sent it on its way around the circle.

I am Jesus, I thought, still wrestling with doubts about my own goodness, *extending my hand to the dregs of the earth.*

I awakened the next morning pondering the status of my journey. I was running out of money, and my hopes of finding a guru were starting to fade.

Where do I go now? I wondered.

As I gazed from the deck of my houseboat at the muddy waters of the Ganges, the only thing clear to me were my feelings of loneliness.

---

11. A wide set of steps descending to a river, especially a river used for bathing.

In my heart of hearts, I knew I was not Jesus, or any other holy man for that matter. I was just a man, alone in the chaos of India, craving the affection of another human being.

I reached for my journal and turned to an entry I'd written years earlier, a quote from a book by Alan Watts.

> Love of nature, love of spirit are paths upon a circle. Only when you travel both at once do you discover this. You must learn to cherish the spirit and the flesh, the angel and the animal. This is the joy, the greatness of being human.[12]

It was all the sanction I needed. The next day, I bought a train ticket for Calcutta. Puri was a small town, Lizzie had told me. I was sure to find her.

---

12. *The Way of Zen* by Alan Watts.

Chapter Thirteen

AFTER A GRUELING TRAIN RIDE FROM Benares to Calcutta, I boarded another train for Puri, 120 miles to the south. Once in Puri, I set out at once to look for Lizzie.

It didn't take long. A German guy at a chai shop responded to my query about a French-Canadian girl by directing me to a fruit stand a mile or two down the road. "She's living in a house fifty meters behind the stand," he said.

Minutes later, I was standing at the door of a small stone cottage. I knocked, hoping it was the right place. The door opened, and there was Lizzie, her eyes and smile as radiant as I'd remembered them.

"Joseph!" she screamed, flinging her arms around my neck. "I knew you'd come! I knew it! Come in...come in!"

I dropped my pack at the entryway and walked with her to a small veranda at the rear of the cottage. The view that met me there was astounding. Never had I dreamed that such a beach could exist in the crowd of India; it was too unlikely, too perfectly untouched to believe.

"How did you *find* this place?" I asked, gaping at the line of breakers that stretched endlessly in the distance. "It's incredible!"

"I met an Indian businessman at the airport in Calcutta," Lizzie explained. "He said he had a summer home in Puri, and that I could rent it from him if I liked. As soon as I saw it, I phoned him and worked out a three-month lease. It's just fifty dollars a month, and it's mine till the end of March. Can you believe it?"

"Wow."

"Yes. And my friends found a place just up the beach. I have this all to myself!"

I didn't say anything.

"Would you like some chai?" Lizzie asked.

"Sure," I said.

Minutes later, Lizzie returned with two cups of chai.

"So, what brings you to Puri?" she asked, handing me one of the cups and sitting beside me on the veranda.

"I think you know why I'm here, Lizzie" I said. "I came to see *you*."

"Yes, yes...I know," she smiled, placing her hand on one of my knees. "I just wanted to hear you *say* it."

We both laughed.

✳✳✳

At first, life in Puri was idyllic. Lizzie painted, while I wrote poetry, plucked on the used guitar I'd found in the Puri marketplace, or carved on the whale's teeth I still had in my possession since Maui. Each day, we swam together in the bay, collected sea shells, or hiked up the beach to a coastline forest teeming with peacocks and white-haired monkeys. In the evenings, we prepared simple meals, then read by lantern light before retiring to the cottage's high-ceilinged bedroom which was furnished only with candles, grass mats, and a four-poster bed draped with mosquito netting. It was a life of exquisite simplicity.

As the days and weeks passed, however, a nagging discontent began to crystallize in my heart. Why was I so antsy? It seemed implausible to be here amid the exotic charm of India, in the company of a beautiful woman, and yet feel so...so *empty*. I was beginning to wonder if "do-nothing" was a higher plane of living or merely an excuse for wasting time.

One day, Lizzie and I were hanging out on the veranda just up from the breakers. Lizzie was at her easel, sketching a small fleet of fishing boats that bobbed several hundred yards offshore. I was reading a book.

Bored with reading, I decided to ask Lizzie a question. A question that had been simmering in my mind for weeks.

"Why did you come to India, Lizzie?" I asked. "I mean, why did you *really* come?"

"Why? What do you mean *why*?" Lizzie said, still concentrating on her canvas.

"I mean, did you come just to paint, to escape the Canadian winter, to find a new lover?"

"Is there anything else?" Lizzie laughed, tilting her head sideways to let the wind lift the hair from her eyes.

"I'm not sure," I said. "That's why *I* came to India—to find out."

"You're too serious, Joseph," Lizzie scoffed, turning to face me. "Don't you remember? You came to India to find *me!*"

"I'm not kidding, Lizzie," I said. "What if we stayed together a few more weeks...a few more months? Don't you want more from life than another short-lived love affair?"

There was a long pause.

"I used to want more," Lizzie smiled. "But I've learned to take what comes. Love is not a matter of time. It's a matter of quality. I can't love more in a year than I can in a day. They say you shouldn't burn your kindling all at once. But why should I stay out in the cold even for one minute?"

"And what happens when love burns out?" I asked.

Lizzie did not answer at first. She just kept dabbing with her paintbrush, adding a sail to one of the fishing boats on her canvas.

"Don't you remember Agra, Joseph?" she finally said. "I told you then...I don't expect too much from life. When it's over, we'll each find someone new. 'After one love, another begins,' remember? Why don't we just enjoy what we have as long as it lasts?"

Suddenly, the magnetic field that had drawn me to Lizzie the moment I met her seemed to disintegrate.

"I'm going for a walk," I said, standing to my feet. "I'll be back by dinner."

For nearly an hour I hiked along the vacant beach to the coastal forest where snow-white monkeys gaped at me from their perches in the trees.

What am I doing? I wondered. I've been in India for nearly three months. But what do I have to show for it? A tan and a soon-to-end relationship.

Just then, I noticed someone approaching me several hundred yards down the beach. *Who could that be?* I wondered. As the figure neared, I could see that it was a sadhu, dressed only in a loin cloth and carrying a long metal trident. Soon, the sadhu was standing directly in front of me. Surprisingly handsome, he had sharp, refined features, long eyelashes, and pearly-white teeth.

"Namaste." I smiled, pressing my palms together in the traditional Indian greeting.

The sadhu did not respond. For several seconds, he just stared at me, his X-ray eyes probing into mine. I felt myself wilting under the heat of his gaze. Then, with the poise of an actor, he lifted his loin cloth.

I could now see that a strange metal contraption was attached to his genitals, a kind of sex-obstructing harness. I was dumbfounded.

Looking up, I saw that the sadhu's eyes were calm and unblinking, and that his teeth formed the nucleus of a knowing grin. Satisfied that he had made his point, the sadhu lowered his loin cloth and, without a word, resumed his long, solitary journey down the beach.

I was immediately convinced that the encounter was no accident. I was also convinced that I understood the sadhu's message: Freedom from the urges of the flesh required discipline. The sadhu's approach was too extreme, of course. But there had to be *some* discipline, *some* path that would work for me. After all, I was in the birthplace of spiritual disciplines!

The next morning I told Lizzie I was leaving. She didn't seem surprised.

Two days later, I stuffed my meager possessions into my backpack and said my final goodbyes.

"Bon soir, Lizzie," I smiled, as we stood together in the doorway of her cottage. "Someday, I hope life gives you more than you expect."

We embraced, and I was on my way.

I had just enough money to buy a one-way train ticket to Calcutta, and from there, a bus ticket to Kathmandu. I had heard about a monastery in Nepal that offered free classes in Tibetan Buddhism. Could this be the path I was looking for?

Sitting alone in the Puri train station, I scribbled a note to my mother. "I feel to be at another major crossroads in my life," I wrote. "I thirst for freedom and inner peace. I'm not so far from the truth, I pray. But the time has come to do at last what will be hard: to stand toe to toe with my life in this world, and work it out."

Soon, as the disciple of a Tibetan Buddhist lama in Nepal, I would have an opportunity to do just that.

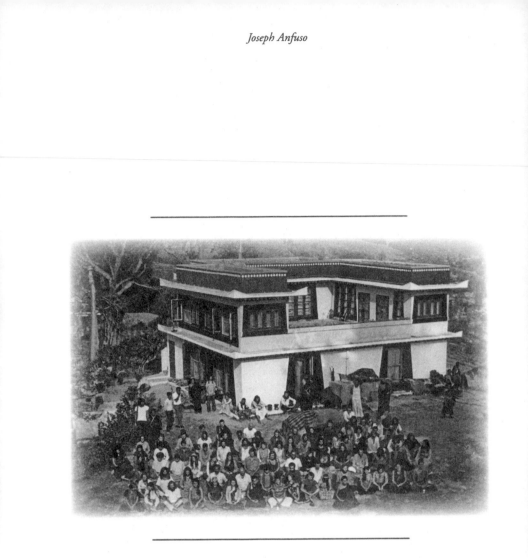

KOPAN MONASTERY IN THE HIMALAYAN FOOTHILLS OUTSIDE
KATHMANDU. I'M IN THE SECOND ROW, SECOND FROM THE LEFT.

Chapter Fourteen

SET ON A LONELY HILLTOP IN the foothills of the Himalayas, Kopan Monastery consisted of a pagoda-style temple, a building where the monks and lamas lived, and a series of small adobe huts where Westerners like myself could take up temporary residence. When I arrived, there were nearly forty Westerners at Kopan, including three French monks, two English nuns, and an assortment of less committed seekers: Americans, Brits, Italians, Australians and French.

From the outset, the routine at Kopan was tedious. Each morning we rose before dawn to climb the steep, switchback trail that led from our huts to the temple, or gompa as it was called, where we gathered for morning meditation. This was followed by breakfast, a bland cereal made from millet called sampa. After breakfast, we returned to the gompa for the first of three daily lectures delivered in surprisingly good English by Thubten Zopa, a wiry, bespectacled lama dressed in crimson and ocher robes. Zopa addressed us from an elevated platform lined with small brass butter lamps and silk-brocade pillows. We sat cross-legged at his feet.

"Craving sensual pleasure is work which has no end," Zopa told us on the day of my arrival. "But teaching of Dharma[13] is work which has an end…work which brings release from suffering and death."

It was a message for which I was primed. After Puri, I was more convinced than ever that sensual pleasure did not satisfy. I had to free myself from the cravings of my flesh, the tyranny of my independent self.

"The principle ignorance is the self-existent 'I,'" Zopa confirmed. "When a man has reached enlightenment, he thinks, 'I am void'—the complete opposite of self-existent 'I.' There is no longer dependence even on the name 'I.'"

---

13. The teaching of the Buddha.

But achieving such loss of self, Zopa warned, would take years, if not lifetimes of effort. "The path is like a rope," he insisted, miming the motions of a man pulling himself upward. "Holding the rope is not sufficient. One must *practice*."

And at Kopan "practice" meant only one thing: a unique form of visualization perfected over many centuries in ancient Tibet.

"Picture in your mind [the great Tibetan holy man] Shakyamuni," Zopa coached. "He is seven forearms in length and perfectly straight, due to good karma of giving away all possessions. His skin is clear and golden, from serving all beings well. His fingernails are pink like coral..." and so on. Once formed, the image was carefully examined, a discipline the lamas believed purified the mind, preparing it for "realizations" and, ultimately, enlightenment.

To motivate us, Zopa spoke frequently of samsara, the endless wheel of birth, suffering and death to which all with uncontrolled desires were bound. "You must see yourself suffering through numberless lifetimes," he urged. "You must see this suffering as unbearable." On one occasion, Zopa told us to picture ourselves boiling in huge vats of oil. "Long-nailed griffins are poking you with white-hot rods, in your ears and in your eyes. You are crying, suffering, pleading for deliverance. You are boiling in those vats for eons...eons without release."

Naturally, I found such images horrifying. After twelve years of Roman Catholic schooling, I'd heard all I wanted to about hell, and had expected more from the high-minded lamas. I also struggled to embrace what appeared to be the "grand prize" of Tibetan Buddhism: oneness with the void. It sounded more like suicide than freedom. But despite my reservations, day after day, week after week, I gave myself sedulously to the lama's teaching.

Finally, after one month at Kopan, Western visitors were invited to participate in a special ordination rite. Participants would be allowed to

A Tibetan monk serves me a bowl of sampa
at Kopan Monastery.

THUBTEN YESHE, KOPAN'S HEAD LAMA.

stay at Kopan to continue their quest for enlightenment. There was just a handful of takers, however, and I was not among them.

On the day of the ceremony I was squatting with two other Westerners just outside the gompa's front screen door. It was just after nightfall, and the hilltop was shrouded by an inky darkness. Inside the gompa, Kopan's head lama, Thubten Yeshe—a barrel-chested man with Mongoloid features, burgundy robes, and a shaven head—sat sternly atop the platform, his legs locked in a full lotus. In his right hand, Yeshe held a Tibetan prayer bell; in his left, a small brass dorje—the Tibetan symbol for lightning. Behind the lama, brightly-colored *thanka* paintings—each depicting a blissful Buddhist master or multi-armed demon—hovered like eerie apparitions. At Yeshe's feet were his initiates, each on one knee, and each holding a cluster of incense sticks.

"Repeat after me," Yeshe instructed, as he guided the initiates through a litany of Tibetan chants.

"Om ah...moga shela...sam bara...bara bara..."

On and on, the lama and his initiates chanted, Yeshe's prayer bell rattling incessantly in his hand. They had been chanting for twenty or thirty minutes when—in perfect English—Yeshe made a strange and unexpected boast.

"When I snap my fingers," he said, "you will feel light and electricity pass through your bodies."

Then the chanting started up again—sam bara...bara bara—and I began to wonder if I had heard what I thought I had.

Just as I was thinking this Yeshe's arm shot outward, his fingers snapping in the darkness.

Instantly, bursts of lightning illuminated the entire hilltop, followed by several claps of thunder. Dumbstruck, I turned to an Australian girl who was squatting to my right. Her face, once hidden in the shadows, was now plainly visible, a mask of disbelief.

And then—as quickly as it had appeared—the lightning vanished, and the hilltop was shrouded again by night.

Peering into the gompa, I saw that Yeshe's eyes were closed, his countenance calm and self-satisfied. The ritual was clearly over.

Later that night, as I lay in my hillside hut, I tried to process what I had just experienced. Ironically, Yeshe's performance had done nothing to fuel my interest in Tibetan Buddhism. More than anything, in fact, it had turned me off. What good had come from the lama's "miracle"? Had anyone been healed? Had a blind man seen? A lame child walked? As far as I could tell, the only beneficiaries were a small group of Westerners, myself included, who now had a story to tell, and an even smaller group, the initiates, who had their faith in Tibetan Buddhism vicariously validated.

But the experience affected me in other ways, too. I was troubled by the fact that my latest attempt to find freedom had led only to another set of standards I could not meet. What hope did I have of meditating for a lifetime, let alone *lifetimes*? It was a realization that left me feeling small, inadequate, not good enough—feelings with which I was all too familiar.

Early the next morning, I headed back to Kathmandu. I wasn't ready to ditch my quest for freedom yet, but after Kopan my sense of what I was capable of doing to free myself was, if nothing else, more realistic.

❋❋❋

I now had four chief objectives: land a job, find a place to live, obtain a long-term visa, and continue my search for a spiritual path. To my surprise and great relief, I managed to accomplish each of these objectives within a matter of days.

First, I found a job as a clerk in a rice paper print shop owned by a Canadian couple who'd been living in Nepal since 1962. Next, I found a room in a house rented by several Californians who had come to Nepal to study Indian music. Then, at the urging of my new friends, I decided to study the sitar, something I hoped might qualify as a spiritual path. And finally, I applied for and obtained a nine-month Nepali visa to study music. Things were looking up!

But my good fortune did not last long. For one thing, the sitar was far more challenging than I anticipated. My first lesson went well enough—perhaps because my teacher wondered if I might be the second coming of George Harrison. But by lesson three, when I still could not play the scales, the smile on his face faded, and I could not bring myself to return for lesson four.

But at least I had my visa. And so, for the next eight months— with no clear plans or purpose or spiritual path—I hunkered down in Kathmandu. My job at the print shop gave me the money I needed to live, and desperate for some form of community, I gradually accumulated a unique menagerie of friends.

There was Shane, a rough-and-tumble Montanan who trotted through Kathmandu on a big white horse. Eight-finger-Eddie, a professional jazz musician who'd been living in the East for ten years and was missing the thumb and forefinger on his right hand. Hugh Raymond Downs, son of the renowned newscaster who was researching a book on Himalayan art. Walking Horse, a forty-something ex-English professor from New York who, as a cohort of Tim Leary and Richard Alpert, had experimented with LSD in the early '60s and now roamed the globe with a kendo stick.[14] And finally, Perry—high school quarterback, amateur guitarist, and irrepressible bundle of energy.

It was Perry, Walking Horse, and I who decided to join forces for what we believed would be "a once-in-a-lifetime adventure": a trek to the base

---

14. Kendo is a Japanese martial art, similar to fencing, in which bamboo swords are used.

camp of Mount Everest. Pooling our resources, we purchased what we knew were the bare essentials—sturdy hiking boots, down sleeping bags, and tinted goggles to protect us from snow blindness at the higher elevations. Base camp was a twelve-day hike from Kathmandu and nearly 18,000 feet above sea level. The trek would be arduous, but, at twenty three, I was fearless and in the best shape of my life. I was stoked.

Two days before heading into the mountains, I was walking along the narrow trail that led from Kathmandu to the house in Swaymabhu where Walking Horse, Perry, and I had been living. It was after nightfall and a half moon provided just enough light to keep me from stumbling. Tall papal and banyan trees hovered on either side of the trail, and now and then I could see my shadow, deceptively taller than my actual height, commingling with the shadows of their branches.

In two days we'll be on our way to Everest, I mused, the adrenaline already pumping in my veins.

I was less than a mile from home when I heard what sounded like a growl coming from the bushes to my right. I turned and saw a mangy dog with huge frenzied eyes and bared teeth gleaming in the moonlight. I froze. For several seconds the dog and I stood motionless. I considered running, then imagined that I was a gunslinger facing down the bad guy on Main Street.

If I hold my ground, I told myself, *he'll back away.*

But he did not back away. He just stood there, the rise and fall of his snarl punctuating the silence like the revving of an engine.

I have to be confident. I can't let him think I'm afraid.

With this in mind, I decided to continue on down the trail. I had barely taken a step when with a single, cobra-like motion the dog sprang forward, plunging his fangs into my leg.

"Damn it!" I screamed as a sharp pain shot up my side. The dog turned, glanced one last time over his shoulder, and disappeared into the night.

THE PHOTO ON MY TREKKING PERMIT FOR THE EVEREST BASE CAMP.

Instantly, I knew three terrible truths: the dog had no owner; it would be impossible to track; and, worst of all, it might be rabid.

Why did this have to happen now?! I groaned.

Minutes later I arrived at our house in Swayambhu. Trying not to favor my leg, I hopped onto the porch and stepped inside.

"Hey, Joe…where you been?" Perry asked, lifting his hand from his guitar to stroke his beard.

"Pickin' up supplies," I said as matter-of-factly as I could.

"You okay?" Perry probed. "You look like something's bothering you."

"No, I'm fine. Just a little tired. I think I'll lie down for a bit."

I crossed the room and climbed the ladder that led to my bedroom loft. I lit my kerosene lamp, pulled up my pant leg, and held the light close to my calf. Two red puncture wounds confirmed my worst fear: the bite had broken the skin. Shaken, I blew out the lamp and spent the rest of that night alone in my loft, unable to sleep.

The next morning, I returned to Kathmandu to see if I could find a book with information on rabies. I found one at Kathmandu's American Library, and what I read was not encouraging.

Symptoms of rabies usually develop between 30 and 90 days after exposure… They include fatigue, muscle aches, anxiety, headache and nausea. Once symptoms appear, it is too late for treatment. When untreated, a human being only survives approximately eight days.

Knowing that I only had four weeks left on my Nepalese trekking permit, I was now faced with a critical decision. If I got rabies shots—a four-week procedure—Perry and Walking Horse would head for Everest without me.

If I did not, I risked contracting a disease that was—100 percent of the time—fatal. I decided to take my chances. Accumulating adventures was all I had going for me at the moment—the only "path" that might someday earn me the love and approval I craved. Two days later, Perry, Walking Horse and I boarded a bus for the Nepali town of Jiri and the trailhead to Everest. If I had rabies, so be it. At least I wasn't sitting on a couch somewhere watching sitcoms or the evening news.

THE CHORTEN AT THANGBOCHE MONASTERY.

Chapter Fifteen

AFTER A NINE-DAY TREK FROM JIRI, I was climbing through a
shadowy forest of tree-like rhododendron and stunted pine. Our
destination that day was Thangboche, a Tibetan Buddhist monastery
13,000 feet above sea level and just three days' hike from the base camp
of Mount Everest.

By now, eight hours into that day's trek, each foot placement had
become a major undertaking and I struggled for air. I experimented with
different methods of breathing, my eyes hunting for the next root or stone
to support me as I pulled myself upward. But nothing seemed to work,
and every forty or fifty feet I slumped exhausted to the ground. Here and
there moss-covered boulders sat like fellow travelers who long before had
fallen beside this trail and then would not, or could not, go on.

Where's Perry? I wondered. I knew Walking Horse was behind me,
or at least I thought he was. But why had Perry raced so far ahead? *Am I
even on the right trail?*

A thick fog began to form around the lower branches of the trees that
lined the trail, first swirling above my head then surrounding me on every
side. I was walking into a cloud. Dampness moistened my hair and beard.

Why is it taking so long? I wondered. And why had no one passed
me along the way? It was so common to see the native Sherpas trudging
along the trails that connected their villages. Where were they?

I struggled to my feet and steeled myself for one more surge upward.
I had barely taken three steps when I saw something manmade, a spire of
some kind, piercing through the fog like the mast of a welcome rescue ship.

It was Thangboche! And the spire part of a large stone monument, or
chorten, where the ashes of dead lamas were interred. Delirious with joy,
I scurried passed the chorten toward the lantern-lit window of a small
wooden shack. I stepped inside and found Perry huddled beside a yak-

dung fire.

"You made it!" Perry groaned, his weary eyes gleaming in the firelight. "That last bit was a killer, wasn't it?"

"You can say that again," I said, tossing my pack to the floor and trying to act nonchalant. "I thought I was on the wrong trail for a minute there." I turned to greet a young Sherpa couple seated on a wooden bench a few feet from the fire. They were clearly our hosts.

"Tah-shi-de-leh," I said, Tibetan for "Hello."

"Tah-shi-de-leh," they replied.

After inhaling a large plate of lentils and rice I crawled into my sleeping bag and, within seconds, was fast asleep.

Next morning, I rose from the hard dirt floor of the shack and opened the smoke-stained shutters above my head. A fresh snow had fallen overnight, and the meadow surrounding the shack was a dazzling white. I pulled on my boots and rushed outside.

The view that met me was astonishing. At the edge of the meadow, like a vision of Shangri-la, was the Thangboche gompa, much larger than Kopan's, with its white-washed walls and pagoda-style roof gleaming in the sunlight. Far above the gompa, and circling the entire meadow, hovered the tallest mountains on earth, including Mount Everest. I was surprised to see that Everest was not the most spectacular of these peaks, nor was it noticeably higher than the rest. Another peak, Amadablam, rose dramatically to the east of Everest and was much more striking.

I pulled up the fur-lined collar of my jacket—a Tibetan monk's robe altered for me by a Kathmandu tailor into a waist-length "parka"—and walked in the direction of the gompa. Midway up the steps that led to the gompa's front door, I turned to face the panorama of peaks. They were breathtaking. But why was I so unimpressed? What did I hope to gain from a trek to Everest? Another story to tell? Another fanciful feather in my cap? Another "accomplishment" that failed to satisfy the deepest, stubborn longings of my heart?

It had also been twelve days since the dog bite, and two lines from the book I'd read before heading for Everest reverberated in my head like drops from a leaky faucet.

"Symptoms of rabies usually develop between 30 and 90 days.... When untreated, a human being only survives approximately eight days."

Fortunately, I had no symptoms yet. But what if they *did* appear? What if my life was draining away like sand in an hour glass?

A bulwark of self-preserving thoughts began to assemble in my head. Had I ever heard of anyone getting rabies in Nepal? What were the odds of *that* dog being rabid? Weren't monkeys the primary transmitters?

But my fears persisted. And as I descended from the gompa steps and made my way back to the shack, I felt oddly detached from the spectacle that surrounded me. I was alone with my fears, alone with my secret, alone with the knowledge that life for me hinged on the presence or absence of a covert infection I could not control.

Walking Horse, Perry, and I would spend the next three days at Thangboche acclimating to the altitude. If we pressed on too soon we risked getting altitude sickness, a condition that could be fatal.

Early on the morning of day three I was awakened by the sound of horns coming from the nearby gompa—the strange, discordant music of the monks. I rose from the floor of the shack and ventured outside. A smoke-like mist was creeping across the meadow as the first rays of sunlight shimmered against the surrounding peaks. I made my way again to the steps of the gompa and turned, as I had before, to face the mountains.

What's wrong with me? I now wondered. My fear of rabies had begun to trigger deeper concerns about the overall condition of my life. I was lonely, aimless, chronically self-absorbed...none of this was hidden from me. Why else had I been so eager to find a spiritual path?

I knew material things were not the answer. And I was also aware, if not convinced, that women were no cure-all either. But what was the antidote? Living in the present? Visualizing Tibetan holy men? Accumulating adventures? As the fitful music of the monks blared across the meadow, the only thing I seemed to know was that I didn't know.

✳✳✳

On the morning of day four at Thangboche, we pressed on toward base camp. Once above the timberline, we hiked for hours along a massive ridge inhabited only by moss-covered shrubbery and hundreds of *mani* stones carved with Buddhist prayers and offered to the sightless wind. We also passed memorials to Western and Sherpa climbers who had died on the slopes of Everest—sobering reminders that not all who passed this way returned.

At last, we came to a tiny village of dreary stone huts. Occupied only part of the year by yak herders, the village—Periche—was a picture of desolation. On the day we arrived, only two huts were occupied, one by an elderly Sherpa woman who welcomed us in.

On entering the woman's hut, we were surprised to find an unlikely store of food lining her shelves. There were cans of ham from America, cans of ravioli from Italy, and cans of soup from Japan. How did they get here? I wondered.

"From expeditions," the Sherpa woman explained, noticing our fascination. "Nepali people no like. Trekkers like."

That night, eager to break our diet of lentils and rice, we feasted on the cans, then retired early to rest for the next day's march toward base camp.

Rising before dawn, we threw on our packs and continued the journey upward. There was nothing now but mountains, snow and sky, the barren landscape stretching before us like an icy desert. When the sun came up, we donned our goggles as protection against snow blindness—an affliction we'd been warned that grated the eyes "like a thousand grains of sand." The higher we climbed, the harder it became, each breath yielding less and less oxygen to our lungs. Soon all conversation ceased, and we concentrated only on the next step.

By midday, we arrived at the last inhabited settlement before base camp: a tiny stone hut where a Sherpa man and his teenage daughter lived. The hut was called Lobuche.

"If you go base camp you need wood," the Sherpa warned soon after our arrival. "You hike base camp, then stay in shelter in middle of glacier. But you need *wood!*"

But we had no wood, and no prospects of getting any. What should we do? That night, as we warmed ourselves beside a smoky yak-dung fire, Walking Horse came up with a plan.

"Why don't we leave our gear in Lobuche and just start hiking?" he coaxed, jabbing his kendo stick into the fire. "It'll be a full moon tomorrow night. Once we reach base camp, we can hike back under the moon!"

"And what if we don't make it back?" Perry asked.

"You don't have to go if you don't want to, Perry," Walking Horse snapped. "What about you, Joe? Are you in?"

I didn't hesitate. "Why not?" I said. "If the weather's good tomorrow morning, we can just start hiking and see what happens."

Next morning, Walking Horse and I headed alone into the glacier in the direction of base camp. We had no tents, no provisions, and no wood. We even left our sleeping bags behind, trusting in our ability to walk back under the moon. What we could not count on, though, were the weather conditions on Everest. They could change in a matter of minutes. And if a storm rolled in—and they frequently did—the odds of us surviving would be slim.

For now, though, the weather conditions were perfect: blue skies, zero wind, and 60 degree temperatures. With the rays of the sun glinting off the ice and snow, Walking Horse and I removed our jackets, wrapping them cavalierly around our waists.

And even more spectacular than the weather was the scenery. Huge snow-capped peaks encircled us on every side, rising 10,000 feet above the 17,000 foot elevation of the glacier. Here and there, great columns of ice, 30 to 60 feet tall, rose from the floor of the glacier like gargantuan popsicles. Adding to the otherworldliness of the glacier was its absolute silence. For nearly an hour I could hear only the beating of my heart and the uniform crunching of my footfalls against the snow.

And then we heard what sounded like an enormous explosion. Walking Horse and I flinched before turning to survey our surroundings. It took several seconds to spot what appeared to be a puff of smoke cascading down the face of a distant peak. It was an avalanche, which though miles away, sounded close enough to sweep us away. There were several more "explosions" after that, and finding each new avalanche became a kind of game.

At last, Walking Horse and I arrived at base camp, a vacant field of ice and snow. It would be years before base camp would become a year-round village, permanently occupied by visiting expeditions. But on this tranquil day in 1973, there was just Walking Horse and me.

"We made it, man! We made it!" Walking Horse whooped, his kendo stick twirling wildly above his head. We found a flat chunk of ice and sat down to rest.

"Not much to look at," I said, scanning the icy rubble that surrounded us.

"What d'ya mean, man? This is *awesome!* How many people can say they've been to Everest?"

"Yeah, I guess you're right," I said.

But with darkness and the temperature falling fast, I was mostly concerned about getting off the glacier alive.

"We better head back," I said.

"Look!" Walking Horse then shouted, pointing his kendo stick over my shoulder.

I turned and saw the dome of the full moon peaking above the saddle between two peaks. It was a welcome sight.

"I told you, man! I told you!" Walking Horse roared.

"We better head back," I repeated. "It took us nine hours to get here. It'll take at least that long to get back."

Hoisting ourselves to our feet, we began retracing our steps toward Lobuche. There was no trail to follow, and no protection against the plummeting temperatures. There was only the moon, the mountains, and the knowledge that somewhere at the far end of the glacier, back where our day had begun, was the warmth and safety of a hut.

It didn't take long for Walking Horse to fall behind. At forty-three, he was twenty years older than me, and not in the best of shape. Concerned for his safety, I repeatedly glanced over my shoulder to make sure he was okay. When I saw his kendo stick wave in big looping circles above his head, I pressed on toward Lobuche.

Look for the light...look for the light, I kept telling myself, thinking of the Lobuche lanterns.

By now, the full moon was directly overhead. If the setting was otherworldly before, it was even more so now. I imagined myself traipsing across a strange, previously undiscovered planet. As the minutes and hours passed, I could not keep my mind from wandering.

You need wood! You need wood! The words of the Sherpa echoed in my head as I pulled the collar of my jacket up tightly around my neck.

Even more persistent were my unrelenting fears about rabies. *When untreated a human being survives only eight days...eight days...eight days...*

And then I flashed on the words of Thubten Zopa at Kopan: "When a man has reached enlightenment, he thinks 'I am void'—the complete opposite of self-existent 'I.'" *I am void...void...void...*

Now, amid the icy vacuum of the glacier, I wondered, as I had at Kopan, if the eastern view of enlightenment was all that appealing. Was "oneness with the void" a fate worth pursuing? And was I, after all my years of wandering, even one step closer to the freedom I craved? Suddenly, the lifeless world of the glacier seemed to mirror the secret, empty landscape of my heart.

What if we can't *find* Lobuche? I now began to fret. Would we have to hike all the way to Periche? That would take hours! And I was already losing strength.

I picked up the pace. But my legs were too weak to handle a faster pace, and now and then I fell face first into the snow. I was just about to panic when I spotted a tiny speck of light flickering in the distance.

Lobuche! I gasped. *That must be Lobuche!*

I turned to check on Walking Horse. He responded with a slow, weary waving of his stick. Thank God, I thought. *We're safe!*

Minutes later, Walking Horse and I were warming ourselves around a smoky, yak-dung fire. My fears and self-doubt had completely vanished.

✳✳✳

Three weeks later, I was sitting with Perry in a restaurant in Kathmandu. It had been four days since our descent from Everest, and twenty-four days since the dog bite. I still had no symptoms, but the faucet in my head continued to drip.

I was concerned, too, about my soon-to-expire Nepali visa. "I can't stay in Nepal much longer," I told Perry, gazing through the restaurant window at a nearby pagoda.

"Why don't we go to India?" he suggested. "There's a big festival in Bodhgaya in a few days…the Dalai Lama's supposed to speak. Why don't we check it out?"

Two days later, Perry and I flew from Kathmandu to northern India. I had no idea that my sojourn in Asia was about to come to an end.

Chapter Sixteen

WE LANDED IN LUCKNOW AND BOARDED a train for Bodhgaya, the birthplace of Buddhism. Here, the Dalai Lama was scheduled to conduct a centuries-old ritual attended by thousands of Buddhist faithful. On the train ride from Lucknow, Perry pulled out a pamphlet he had been given in Kathmandu detailing the ritual. I listened intently as he read aloud.

According to Buddhist tradition, an important body of teachings was given by Buddha himself to a small group of initiates in South India. For centuries the teachings had been transmitted orally from master to carefully chosen disciple. Eventually, around 1100 A.D., the teachings were brought across the Himalayas to Tibet where they were handed down, century after century, in an unbroken lineage.

"Are you following this?" Perry asked, looking up.
"Yeah," I said. "Keep reading."
Perry lowered his head and continued.

Originally, in Tibet, the teachings were propagated only among the priestly lamas and concealed from the common people. But then, around the turn of the eighteenth century, a tradition was established whereby each Dalai Lama dispensed the teachings publicly, presenting them during an eight-day ritual. Just to be present at the ritual is considered an important step on the path to enlightenment.

"Wow, do you think that's really true?" Perry asked, looking up. "I mean, the part about getting closer to enlightenment?"
"I have no idea," I said. "But I don't see why it would push us further away."

Stepping from the train in Bodhgaya, we could see at once that the festival, or wang as it was called, was a bigger deal than we had anticipated. There were pilgrims everywhere, more than a hundred thousand, most encamped in a "city" of elaborately-embroidered tents. There were pilgrims from Japan, Tibet, Bhutan, Ladakh and Sikkim. I remember thinking that it was an Asian Gathering of the Tribes, only four times bigger and much more colorful.

After traversing the tent city, Perry and I came to the towering obelisk, or stupa, that marked the spot where Buddha had achieved enlightenment 500 years before Christ. Nearly 200 feet tall, the stupa rose from the flat surrounding landscape like a prehistoric rocket. Hundreds of prayer-wheel-spinning pilgrims prostrated themselves around the base of the stupa, one body length at a time, like human inch worms.

"This should be interesting," Perry said, as we surveyed the colorful pilgrims.

It better be more than that, I groaned inwardly. I was just about burned out on "interesting."

Three days later, Perry and I were sitting again by the stupa trying to process our experience. On each of the previous three days, hordes of pilgrims had gathered in a field not far from the stupa as the Dalai Lama dispensed his teachings from beneath a large, brightly-embroidered canopy that shielded him from the sun.

"Are you getting anything out of this?" I asked Perry.

"Only if that thing about 'just being present' is true," he smiled. "I mean, we can't understand a single word! And even if we could, I'm not sure it would make any difference."

"So...what do you want to do?" I asked.

"I don't know," Perry sighed. "What do *you* want to do?"

"All I know is my Indian visa runs out in two weeks, and if I don't

THE STUPA AT BODHGAYA, INDIA.

get a new one, I may have to return to the States."

"Is that so bad?" Perry asked.

The question caught me off guard. I had to think for a few seconds before answering.

"Not necessarily," I said. "It's just that I've been living in India and Nepal for more than a year now, and what do I have to show for it? One failed relationship, and some far-out experiences."

"So?"

"So, is that all there is? Just more wandering...more relationships... more far-out experiences? I came here to find truth, Perry. A path I could believe in. And so far I've only found one sick guru, an invitation to spend lifetimes meditating, and some lectures I can't understand!"

Perry stared at the stupa with a pained look in his eyes. Several seconds passed; and then, as if speaking to himself, he uttered a single, mysterious word.

"Goenka."

"Goenka? What's that?" I asked.

"A Burmese guru," Perry said, turning to face me. "He teaches a meditation technique, something to do with watching your breath. I met some of his followers in Kathmandu just before we left for India. According to them he's not your typical guru...just a guy who teaches this technique you're free to do with what you want. It sounds a lot like TM."[15]

I had just about had my fill of gurus, sadhus and sages, but the idea of spirituality without religion appealed to me.

---

15. Transcendental Meditation (TM) is a form of meditation introduced in India in 1955 by Maharishi Mahesh Yogi, the guru of The Beatles. The technique involves the use of a sound or mantra and is practiced for 15–20 minutes twice per day while sitting comfortably with closed eyes.

POSING FOR A PHOTO ON MY WAY TO THE GOENKA COURSE. I AM ON
THE LEFT, PERRY IS IN THE MIDDLE.

"Does he live near here?" I asked.

"I don't know where he lives. But he's giving a ten-day course in Allahabad in a few days. We could take the train…"

Two days later, Perry and I were riding together in a rickshaw on our way to the venue for Goenka's "course," a walled-in compound not far from Allahabad's city center. When we arrived at the compound we found four hundred people, mostly Westerners, gathered in a large, multi-colored tent. Goenka, a dark-skinned man with bulging cheeks and snow-white hair, was addressing the group from a platform near the front of the tent.

"The purpose of my teaching is to help you discover the truth within yourselves," he declared, in perfect English, just as Perry and I entered the tent. "You must go deep inside, to the deepest levels of the mind. Only in this way can you eradicate the impurities of the mind, and gain enlightenment.

"The yardstick for success is freedom from reaction," Goenka continued. "The whole of our meditation is to keep the mind balanced, knowing full well that things keep on changing. We have just to observe the chemistry and physics of the body, the electro-magnetic reactions taking place every moment, without identifying them as 'I,' 'me,' 'mine.'

"The goal is to keep balance of mind in spite of all vicissitudes, the ups and downs of life. I get pleasant situations or painful situations; I get victories or defeats; I get profits or losses; I get good names or bad names—I am bound to face all these things. But can I smile in every situation?"

The key to achieving this balance, Goenka insisted, was a breathing technique he called "Vipassana."

"Our breath is the bridge between the known and the unknown," he said. "Mental defilements make the breath rough and hard. You must concentrate to eliminate this wavering."

As I listened to Goenka's teaching, I was reminded of what I had heard at Kopan about purifying the mind, dissolving the self and, most of all, practice, practice, practice. Spiritual freedom, I now assumed, could only be achieved through some form of personal effort. *So why not Vipassana?* At least there were no butter lamps or thanka paintings.

And so, for the next five days, I devoted myself to the practice of Vipassana. On days one through three—from five in the morning until seven at night—I focused on my nostrils: "in breath...out breath... natural breath...bare breath" and so on.

On day four, I shifted to my face, neck, shoulders and arms.

"Simply observe," Goenka coached. "Observe and be vigilant."

On day five, I started to lose it. Fortunately, a break was scheduled for that evening and several course attendees, including Perry and me, were gathered around a small bonfire in a corner of the compound not far from the tent. Most around the fire were veterans of Goenka's teaching, their stoic expressions and self-assured air giving them away. The atmosphere was stilted, and there was little or no conversation. Finally, with characteristic spontaneity, Perry pulled out his guitar and began to sing.

"I left my happy home...to see what I could find out...I left my folk and friends...with the aim to clear my mind out..."

Though only an average musician, Perry had a knack for strumming the guitar that usually got everyone's toes tapping—bouncy, upbeat rhythms that only a prig could hate—all the while keeping a broad, irresistible grin on his face.

I glanced around the fire to gauge the response of Goenka's followers. Most were blank-faced, and though some seemed to enjoy Perry's music, only a few managed smiles. *Was this the freedom Goenka's teaching produced?*

Later that night, back in my "meditation cell," I was bombarded with doubts. The closer I looked at eastern religions, it seemed, the less attractive they became. By now I had read dozens of books on the subject; visited ashrams and retreat centers in California and Hawaii; and fancied myself a bona fide seeker in the eastern tradition. And yet, in the very cradle of eastern mysticism, I was starting to feel disillusioned.

But what else is there? I wondered. And, with only eight days left on my Indian visa, I feared returning to the States no wiser or more enlightened than I had left.

Desperate to have at least *something* in my spiritual "tool box," I decided to finish Goenka's course. I wasn't sold on Vipassana, but it was at least the closest thing I had found to an acceptable path.

✳✳✳

At the end of Goenka's course, Perry headed for Bali, and I for New Delhi where I hoped to renew my Indian visa. Almost broke, I could only afford a tiny, box-like room on the rooftop of a flea-bag hotel. It was just after sunset, the day before I planned to renew my visa, and I was sitting cross-legged on a cot in my "hotel room." The bare light bulb on the ceiling was off, and I was surrounded by a shadowy dusk.

With my eyes closed, I tried to focus on my breath—in breath, out breath—then shifted my focus from the top of my head to my face... neck...shoulders...arms. At the outset, the sound of rickshaw bells, taxi horns and high-pitched Indian music blared loudly from the street below. Soon, the street noise faded, and there was only the soft, steady beating of my heart.

And then, for no apparent reason, I opened my eyes. Still observing, I watched as the top horizontal and mid-vertical boards of my hotel-room door became illuminated in the form of a cross. I found myself squinting to shield my eyes. I then had a simple, entirely unexpected thought: It's Jesus...*Jesus* is the way.

Then the cross receded, as quickly as it had appeared. I was back in the darkness of my hotel room, and the cocoon of silence that had enveloped me was shattered by the sound of rickshaw bells and Indian music blaring on the street below. I was back in India—as far from the symbols and culture of Christianity as I had ever been in my life.

The next day my request for a new Indian visa was flatly denied. And two days later, after accepting an offer from my brother Vic of a one-way plane ticket back to the States, I was soaring westward toward New York City. What awaited me there would change my life.

—

Chapter Seventeen

VIC HAD ALWAYS BEEN A KIND of surrogate father to Frank and me. Seventeen years our senior, he was old enough to keep us in line, but young enough to be our friend. Among our favorite childhood memories, in fact, were the times Vic took us on skiing trips to New England when he would wake us before dawn for the long drive north and treat us to overnight stays at local hotels. During his law school years, Vic would sequester himself in his room on the second floor of our Brooklyn brownstone, coming out only for meals or to use the bathroom. But even then he found time to wrestle with us on the floor of his room, bouts that always ended with him on top and Frank or me begging for him to get off. Now, at forty, Vic had his own Manhattan law firm and lived with his wife, Kathy, and their two children (they would eventually have five) on the north shore of Long Island.

When I landed at JFK, Kathy was the one who picked me up. Tall, gregarious and self-assured, Kathy was the daughter of prominent New York attorney, Bill Shea. A household name in New York, Mr. Shea had negotiated the deal that brought the Mets to town, an achievement that resulted in their stadium bearing his name. I remember as a junior at Rutgers picking up an issue of *New York Magazine* that featured a cover story on Bill Shea. The story was titled: "The Most Powerful Man in New York."

"Good to see you again, Joe," Kathy smiled as I tossed my backpack into the trunk of her Lincoln Continental. "It's been a long time."

"Almost two years," I said as I slid into the passenger-side seat. "How are things on the home front?"

There was a brief pause.

"Actually, there have been some very exciting changes, Joe," Kathy said mysteriously. "We can't wait to tell you about them."

Changes?

I was about to assure her of changes in my own life when we merged onto the Van Wyck Expressway and accelerated to 60 miles per hour. After nearly two years in Asia, getting around mostly on foot or in rickshaws, a New York City freeway was all it took to send me into culture shock. For the next thirty minutes, with my hands braced against Kathy's dashboard, I listened distractedly as she updated me on her children, New York City politics, and the state of the Union.

At last we arrived at Vic and Kathy's home, a twenty-two room Tudor set amid tall oak and elm trees on Long Island's "gold coast." Clean, roomy and finely appointed, it was everything India was not, and the contrast was jarring. *How will I adjust to my new surroundings?* I wondered. And what were the "changes" Kathy had alluded to?

That night, after settling into a guestroom in Vic's attic, I joined Vic, Kathy and my Mom—who now lived with Vic and Kathy—at a sumptuously-set table in Vic's dining room. Surrounding me on every side were the musts of a privileged lifestyle: French country furniture, Crown Darby silverware with bone-china handles, a painting by famed Italian artist, Giorgio de Chirico, and in the middle of the table, a large Limoges centerpiece filled with freshly-cut peonies. It was as if I'd fallen asleep in an Indian flophouse and awakened in a princely estate.

"So, tell us about your travels, Joe," Vic queried, handing me a platter of T-bone steaks. "What was it like in India and Nepal?"

"Well, I…I'm not sure where to begin, Vic," I said. "There's so much to tell."

"I'm sure. But what about the spiritual side…is it as dark over there as they say?"

"Dark?"

"Yes, you know…demon worship, false gods, that sort of thing."

I detected an unforeseen boldness in Vic's question, as if he were setting me up for some kind of metaphysical debate. I parried back.

"Well, I don't know…I didn't find it dark. Actually, it was more enlightening than dark." And then, glancing at the De Chirico, I said, "It sure taught me how little I need to be happy."

"Yes, I know what you mean," Kathy interjected. "We're finding that out ourselves."

I was getting irritated now. For years I had seen Vic and Kathy as pillars of the establishment, materialists, with no real interest in things spiritual. *I* was the spiritual seeker, the globetrotting mystic, the pilgrim in search of truth. But now, as they stared at me across their dining room table, there was a disturbing confidence in their eyes, and I wondered why.

"We might as well tell you, Joe," Vic then said, like a schoolboy blurting out a secret. "We want to hear all about your travels; we really do. But when you're finished we hope you'll let us tell you what happened to us. Kathy and I have found Jesus, Joe. We've found a personal relationship with Jesus Christ, and it's changing our lives."

I was speechless. Vic and Kathy? *Jesus freaks?*

"And we're not the only ones," Vic continued. "There's George and Maria, and Diana…Mother, too."

I turned to Mom.

"That's right, Joe," she smiled. "You're the only one now. The only one."

✳✳✳

Over the next twenty-four hours I listened intently as Vic and Kathy explained what had happened. They told me how Frank had flown from California to New York weeks earlier to tell them about his newfound faith in Jesus. They shared about the struggles they had been having in their marriage, and the "marriage encounter" they'd attended at the invitation of a friend. And finally, they described how over a period of just six weeks, Mom and all my older siblings had "accepted Jesus as their personal Lord and Savior."

Naturally, I was shocked. But the news might have been less troubling were it not for the fact that implicit in all they said was the belief—clear from the outset—that Jesus was "the only way." And while they were willing to hear my stories, they showed little or no interest in my spiritual beliefs. Jesus was The Answer. Period. End of subject.

I was now confronted by a serious problem: How could I stay true to my own convictions while at the same time stay connected to my family? Admittedly, I had spent most of the previous four years physically separated from my family, but I still felt a strong and enduring bond with them, a bond I was loathe to break. It was also quite evident that my family *loved me*, and the prospect of disappointing not just Frank but everyone else in my family seemed to hover above my head like the Sword of Damocles.

Less than a week after my arrival in New York, Vic called me into his bedroom.

"Frank asked me to give this to you," he said, handing me a small white cassette tape. "He thinks you should listen to it when no one's around."

That night, alone in my attic room, I inserted the tape into the small black recorder Vic had loaned me and pressed the play button. There were several seconds of static. Then the soft, ethereal voice of my twin.

"The Lord has given me some songs to share with you, Joe," Frank began, almost in a whisper.

Songs? *Frank?* Since when does he know how to sing? I turned up the volume.

"I hope you'll listen with an open heart," Frank continued. And then, in the folksy, acoustic style of the 1960s, he began to sing.

"Lend an ear of faith…there is a message…a tale of life unseen that is soo real…"

Is that Frank? I gasped. *Where did he learn to sing like that?!* I felt as if I was listening to a stranger.

"Yes, Jesus, you're the only one I'm after. You're the only one I ever really wanted to know…I love you so."

With each successive song I found myself marveling at the freedom in Frank's voice, the sincerity, the heartfelt conviction. Hid away in Vic's attic, I reflected back on my just-ended journey to the East. I pictured myself sitting with Lizzie on the beach in Puri…meditating with the lamas at Kopan…trudging across the glacier between Lobuche and base camp. And while each mental picture was different, the same theme of frustration connected them like a palm connects the fingers of an empty hand. I was suddenly and painfully aware that there was no music in my heart, no song of freedom, no "tale" aching to be told. By the final song on Frank's cassette, tears coursed slowly down my face, and I wasn't sure why.

✳✳✳

I now decided to examine more closely the claims of Christianity. With no job and no nearby friends, I had plenty of time on my hands. And if nothing else, I owed it to my family to seriously consider their assertions. I did not foresee any challenges. After twelve years of Roman Catholic schooling, I considered myself well acquainted with Christianity. I was also comfortable with the idea that Jesus was a great teacher, one of many "fully realized beings" who had lived over the centuries. It was the assertion that he was unique—the *only* way to God—that I could not accept. I felt confident, then, that I could synthesize the fundamental tenets of Christianity with the other spiritual teachings I had explored along the way.

And so, for the first time in my life, I began to read the Bible.[16] I

---

16. As a Roman Catholic growing up in the 1950s, I was strongly discouraged from reading the Bible. Bible study was the province of priests, and ordinary believers were virtually prohibited from delving into the scriptures on their own.

started with the Gospel of John, followed by the other gospels, the letters of the New Testament, and finally, the Old Testament books of Genesis, Psalms, Proverbs and Ecclesiastes. To my surprise, I found them less oblique than I had expected. And the more I read, the more I realized that this strange, intriguing book did not fit as neatly into my belief system as I had expected.

For one thing, I found undeniable consistency in the story of Jesus Christ. The account was vivid, comprehensible, and yes—unique. Pretending I did not understand the basic story would have been disingenuous.

But there was one aspect of the story that left me baffled: the repeated and inscrutable reference to "blood." First, the blood of animals sprinkled on altars by Old Testament Jews; then the blood of Jesus shed centuries later on the cross. Throughout the clear, well-reasoned pages of the New Testament, blood seemed splattered like some crude, anti-intellectual clue.

Gradually, I found myself forced to concede that any attempt to squeeze the Bible's message into my own preconceptions would have been a violation of the authors' clear intent. And the more I read, the more it seemed that I either had to believe the story—something I could not imagine myself doing—or reject it as a foolish fabrication.

Interesting book, the Bible," I reluctantly concluded. *Interesting book.*

"Hey, Joe," Vic announced one morning over breakfast. "I got a phone call last night from an old friend of yours. I think you knew her in California. She lives in Brooklyn now. Do you remember a German woman named Sabine Ball?"

Chapter Eighteen

I REMEMBERED SABINE, OF COURSE. THAT last night in Mendocino, when she had joined us in the sharing-time circle at Table Mountain, was still vivid in my mind. I remembered her telling us about her childhood in Nazi Germany, her ill-fated marriage to a Miami millionaire, and her dropping out to California. More than anything, I recalled her startling admission that she had "found Jesus," and the ice-cold reception this had received. *Why had this once revered seeker embraced such a narrow-minded path?* I recalled wondering at the time. And now I wondered why she had moved from Mendocino to Brooklyn of all places? (This was decades before Brooklyn would become a magnet for 21st Century hipsters.)

I decided to pay her a visit. Vic told me that she was living in a Christian commune not far from Williamsburg. Hiking passed littered, empty lots and dilapidated brownstones, I reflected back on the beauty of Mendocino, with its quaint, wood-framed cottages, towering redwoods and pristine beaches. *What on earth was Sabine doing here?* I marveled.

At last I arrived at a brownstone that matched the address Vic had given me: 24 Prospect Place. Wedged between equally-rundown buildings, the brownstone was distinguished only by a small, brightly-painted sign that hung above the front door. "The Shepherd's House." I climbed the brownstone's stoop and rang the doorbell. The door opened, and a tall, earnest-looking guy with blond hair and freckles greeted me warmly.

"Why, hello!" he piped. "Can I help you?"

"My name's Joseph," I said guardedly. "Does a woman named Sabine live here?"

"Why, yes," he beamed. "Come in! Come in!"

Treating me like an old friend, he ushered me into a large high-ceilinged room with secondhand furniture pushed flat against the walls. It looked like a room used for meetings.

"Say, you wouldn't be related to Vic Anfuso, would you?" he then asked, apparently tipped off about my impending visit.

"Yes," I said. "He's my older brother."

"Is that right!" he crowed, sounding like a sawdust preacher. "I know Vic! He's a great guy. A real man of God. And you're his brother, you say!"

I watched as his earnest eyes darted incredulously from my beard to my turquoise and coral earring and finally my Tibetan jacket with the stand-up collar. *I don't think he's one of us,* I could almost hear him thinking.

"Why don't you sit right there and I'll get Sabine for you." He smiled, pointing to a sofa that faced a steep, narrow stairwell.

I took a seat and surveyed my surroundings. Apart from its mish mash of furniture, the interior of the brownstone was remarkably nondescript. There was only a small wooden cross in the foyer and a framed embroidery on one wall that read: "For the ways of man are before the eyes of the Lord, and He ponders all his paths" (Proverbs 5:21). I could not stop marveling that a woman like Sabine would live in a place like this.

Just then Sabine descended the stairwell, dressed in what appeared to be a maid's uniform: navy blue dress, white apron and matching white cap. I was stunned. Sabine...*a maid?*

"Ah, Joseph," she smiled, her German accent adding a touch of class to her greeting. "I was told you might be coming. Please excuse my attire. I just got home from work."

"Hello, Sabine," I said, standing up to greet her. "It's good to see you again."

"Yes, yes, it's been a while, I think," she said, sitting down beside me on the couch. "What have you been up to, Joseph?"

"Actually, I just returned from Asia a couple weeks ago. I spent almost two years there…mostly in India and Nepal."

"Really? I was in Nepal, you know…back in 1968. I spent three months there… two in a Tibetan Buddhist monastery."

"Oh? Which monastery?"

"It was just outside Bodhnath…a place called Kopan. Do you know it?"

I could hardly believe my ears.

Suddenly, the chasm that had always distanced me from "less experienced," "less sophisticated" Christians seemed to evaporate. *I know where you're coming from, Joseph,* Sabine's eyes seemed to assure me. And I felt strangely uncomfortable.

"So…how is Lama Yeshe?" Sabine then asked. "Is he still there?"

"Uh…yes…he's still there," I muttered. "He's doing well, I think."

"Ah, that's good to hear. I was quite impressed with him, you know."

"Yes. He's an amazing man."

"And what did you learn in the East, Joseph?" Sabine then probed, not contentiously, but with what seemed like genuine curiosity.

I proceeded to summarize my many adventures, leaving out my tryst with Lizzie, and emphasizing the spiritual nature of my journey: my stay at Kopan…my study of the sitar…my visit to Bodhgaya, and the meditation course with Goenka. Sabine listened with no hint of judgment or disapproval.

We were then interrupted by two giggling children who ran into the room and jumped playfully onto Sabine's lap. I seized the opportunity to escape.

"Well, I better be goin', Sabine," I said, standing up to leave. "It's been nice visiting with you."

"Yes, it's been nice," Sabine smiled. "Let me walk you to the door."

I was just about to exit when Sabine asked a final, disconcerting question.

"Joseph…why don't you ask God to show you if he's real? He can do that, you know. He knows everything about you. And he wants to reveal himself. Why don't you ask *him*?"

For some reason, Sabine's question bypassed my defenses.

"I just might do that someday, Sabine," I said, seemingly against my will. "I just might do that."

***

One week later, I was sitting cross-legged on my bed in Victor's attic. It was nearly midnight, and the room was shrouded in darkness. For more than an hour I'd been trying to meditate, slowly shifting my attention from my head…to my neck…shoulders…chest… And then I opened my eyes. Light from a street lamp seeped through a crack in the curtains on the opposite side of the room.

Was it possible? I wondered.

I rose from my bed and stepped gingerly to the center of the room.

"Why don't you ask *him*?" Sabine's question echoed softly in the back of my head.

I knelt down, closed my eyes, and began to pray. Odd, I thought, that after all my wild experiences these past few years that praying to the God of the Bible should seem strange.

"If you're there," I began, nearly smiling at the absurdity of it all, "show me if you're real. Yes, I want to know. Show me if you're real."

Chapter Nineteen

THREE NIGHTS LATER, WHILE ASLEEP IN Vic's attic, I had a dream.
I knew immediately where I was. It was Bodhgaya, the birthplace
of Buddhism. All around me, turbaned men and saried women ran
screaming through the streets, their arms waving wildly above their heads.
As I ambled amid the chaos, I seemed to be invisible, yet fully present.

Where is the stupa? I wondered.

And then I saw it…or what remained of it. It was nothing now but
rubble, barely one stone left standing atop another. The sky, once hidden
by the towering obelisk, was now clearly visible, dark and foreboding.

Desperate to find shelter, I ducked into a nearby hut. As soon as I
entered I was confronted by a creature of some kind, goat-like, but much
more menacing. It was trying to hurt me…to kill me…to force me under!

And then I woke up.

What was that about? I gasped, as I peeled back my sheets and
switched on the light beside my bed. My first instinct was to dismiss the
dream as nothing but a food-induced nightmare. But it was too vivid,
too seemingly purposeful for that. And besides, the dream's message was
too obvious to be totally ignored.

It was a warning about my spiritual quest. The stupa—reaching
heavenward like an outstretched arm—was a symbol of my attempts
to seek enlightenment with my own wisdom and strength. And its
destruction—along with the presence of an evil creature—conveyed
the risk and inauspicious outcome of my pursuit. I resisted this
interpretation, of course. But I could not help but wonder if the dream
might have been an answer—unwelcome though it might be— to my
Sabine-inspired prayer.

Two days later, I paid another visit to the Shepherd's House. The
dream had fueled my interest in Christianity, and I was willing if not

eager to examine it more closely.

"Good to see you again, Joseph!" the blond guy with freckles greeted me again when I arrived. "Please join us!"

Once inside, I could see that twenty or thirty people were gathered in the living room for what appeared to be an informal church service. A small man with a scraggly red beard and Scottish brogue was addressing the group from a chair on the far side of the room. I sat cross-legged on the floor directly in front of a large, balding man with anchors tattooed on his forearms.

"And so, when the son sets you free," the Scotsman screeched, a big black Bible in his lap, "you're free indeed!

"All of us yearned for freedom at some time or other in our lives," he continued. "Some of us traveled; some took drugs or dabbled in eastern religions. But in the end, all our attempts to get free left us only tense and unfree. Instead of freeing ourselves, we got more trapped, more entangled in half-truths and lies.

"That's because freedom—true spiritual freedom—comes only one way: by surrendering our lives to Jesus Christ. When a person does this, they let something wonderful happen to them. Instead of being wiped out—the way devotees of eastern religion sometimes are—they become what Jesus called 'born again.' The only thing wiped out is the false self they had built up. Suddenly, they don't have to prove anything to anyone, or play a part; they can, at last, be themselves."

There was something oddly authoritative about the Scotsman. He was obviously intelligent and surprisingly articulate—observations accentuated no doubt by my less-than-high expectations. I was impressed. And when he was done speaking, I crossed the room to introduce myself.

"I enjoyed your presentation," I said, a hint of condescension in my voice.

"Thank you," the Scotsman smiled.

"There's just one thing that bothers me."

The smile on the Scotsman's face did not falter.

"Why do you guys insist that Jesus is the *only* way? Can't you just follow his teachings without implying that every other teaching is inferior, even false? I find that offensive."

The Scotsman hesitated for a moment, and then fixed me with a steady gaze. "Because Jesus *is* the only way," he said calmly. "You see, the world's religions claim that we can find God, that we can be acceptable to God, even become God, by means of our own wisdom and strength. We just have to be good enough, holy enough, try hard enough.

"But the Bible says just the opposite is true—or at least the New Testament does. Instead of saying we have to be good enough to find God, it says we can only find him by abandoning our own works, by accepting by faith what he has already done for us."

"And what's that?" I interjected.

The Scotsman hesitated again, his eyes angling downward and then rising to meet mine.

"He sent his son," he said, as if the enormity of the thought had struck him for the first time. "Not with pomp or ceremony—the way we might have sent him. But as an ordinary man, the son of a carpenter. The Bible says he was equal with God, but he made himself nothing, taking on the form of a servant and living a life of utter obedience. For thirty-three years he faced every temptation known to man, yet never once acted selfishly. Then, after he'd done nothing but good, he was put to death—and the death he died was that of a common criminal.

"It was this sacrifice, the Bible says, and the resurrection that followed, that changed the course of history. By paying the just penalty for man's sins, Jesus became the savior of the world. Now, instead of having to earn God's approval or find spiritual freedom on the basis of our own works—something none of us can do—we can come to God on the basis of what Jesus did for us—something anyone can do.

"If there's another spiritual path anything like this," the Scotsman concluded, "I've never heard of it. And frankly, I don't believe it exists."

The Scotsman fell silent now, and I sensed that others in the room were listening in on our conversation.

"But how can you be so sure?" I snapped. "How do you know you're right?"

"Oh, I can't convince you," he smiled. "It's something you have to experience for yourself. Jesus said, 'If any man *chooses* to do God's will, he will know the teaching, whether it comes from God or whether I speak for myself.' God never *makes* us respond to his message…we have to *choose* to respond."

Just then, I noticed that the large tattooed man I'd been sitting in front of was staring at me from a nearby sofa. He had clearly been eavesdropping on our conversation. I excused myself from the Scotsman and stepped over to introduce myself.

"My name's Joseph," I said warily. I could now read the words "Todd's Shipyard" on the big man's shirt. *He must be a longshoreman.*

"My name's Robert," the big man grinned, his eyes targeting me like spotlights. I was suddenly aware of my earring, my Rasputin-like beard, my Tibetan jacket with the stand-up collar and my handmade moccasins.

"Ya know, dare's sumptin' I been wantin' ta ayx you," he then said, in one of the thickest Brooklyn accents I had ever heard.

"Oh. What's that?"

"Why don't ya just get auf yer trip?"

I reeled back, dazed. It was as if a mask had been ripped from my face. I knew instantly that there was nothing about my carefully-crafted persona—my colorful outfit, spiritual insights or fanciful adventures—

that would ever impress the simple, honest man who now confronted me. I felt naked in his presence.

"Ah…well…I'm not sure I know what you mean," I stammered, fumbling for something to say. But there was nothing to say. The man had made his point, and I was speechless.

Shaken, I fled into the nearby kitchen to see what time it was. *Ten thirty!* The last train for Long Island left Penn Station in fifteen minutes. There was no way I could make it.

Begrudgingly, I asked the Scotsman if I could spend the night. "Of course you can! There's an empty bed in the brother's dorm."

Five hours later I was lying awake on a bunk bed in the Shepherd's House "brother's dorm." The others in the room were fast asleep, and fearful of waking them, I exploited the wail of a passing siren to muffle the shifting of my body under the sheets. Staring into the darkness, I found myself battling the authenticity of the big man's challenge: *Why don't ya just get auf yer trip?*

Like lava in a volcano, three words suddenly began to force themselves uncontrollably toward my throat: I give up…I give up…*I give up!*

I was just about to shout these words into the brother's dorm when I pictured myself surrounded by a swarm of bible-thumping evangelists. It was enough to jolt me back to my senses. For the moment at least, an eruption had been thwarted. But it was just a matter of time, I now suspected, before the caricature I had fashioned for myself would collapse. And I wondered who or what would take its place?

Chapter Twenty

FOUR DAYS LATER, ON MARCH 23, 1974, I was sitting in the living room of my sister Maria's home on Long Island. It was here, two years earlier, that I had made my final preparations for the overland journey to India. Now, less than two months after returning to the States, I was back in the same room, only this time in the company not only of Maria and George, but Victor, Kathy, and a young Christian minister from New Hampshire named Dave.

For more than an hour, I had been listening as Vic, George and Dave meandered through a wide range of topics, from baseball and politics to the birthplace of St. Patrick—northern England, they finally agreed, not Italy as Vic had jokingly insisted. It was a pleasant conversation, full of laughter, openness and mutual respect. How I longed for what I saw in these men—their candor, their spontaneity, their lack of self-consciousness. Whatever they were not, they were, at least, *themselves*.

It had been over 91 days since the dog bite, and the faucet of fear about rabies was now turned off. But a bigger faucet—the nagging awareness that my life lacked direction, meaning or higher purpose—was still dripping inside my head. Was it time to turn that one off, too?

"Excuse me," I blurted, leaning forward in my seat.

Every eye turned in my direction.

"I want to give my life to Jesus," I said.

A deafening silence filled the room. *Is he serious?* they seemed to be asking themselves. Up until now, I had given no indication of leaning toward faith in Jesus, let alone surrendering to him.

But their incredulity did not last long.

"That's wonderful, Joe," Dave said. "Why don't we gather around you and you can repeat this prayer after me."

And so, with Dave's help, I repeated the following prayer.

"Lord Jesus...I invite you into my life...I admit that I am a sinner... that all my life I have been living for myself, and not for you....Thank you for forgiving my sins... and for dying on the cross to set me free...I open the door of my heart to you...I accept you as my personal Lord and Savior...Amen."

No sooner had I prayed this then the entire room erupted in a chorus of "Hallelujahs!" Tears flowed freely down Maria's face as she, George and Victor embraced me with heartfelt hugs.

"You should call Francis in California!" Maria exclaimed, handing me the headset of her living room phone. "He'll be so excited!"

I dialed Frank's number. The phone rang once or twice, and then I heard the voice of my twin.

"I just accepted Jesus, Frank," I told him after a brief greeting.

"Praise God! Praise God!" he screamed, then shouted the news to others who were apparently with him in the room. Another chorus of "Hallelujahs!"—this time barely audible—echoed faintly through the phone line. After some additional congratulatory comments from Frank, we said our goodbyes and I hung up the phone.

It was, in every respect, a joyous celebration. Except for one thing...I felt none of my family's joy. I mostly felt embarrassment—like a soldier waving a white flag above his head. Someday, I thought, I might share their enthusiasm, their certainty, their unbridled joy. For now, though, I would have to settle for bringing them all happiness.

That night, asleep in Victor's attic, I would have another dream. Once again, I was back in Asia, this time in Periche, the remote Himalayan village two days' hike from the base camp of Mount Everest. High above the timberline and encircled by snow-capped peaks, the village—nothing but a cluster of huts—was just as I remembered it: a picture of desolation. Only this time, it had not just taken days to get there, but years. I felt anxious, exhausted, and painfully alone.

Just then I spotted a column of smoke billowing in the distance. *"Life!"* I thought as I scurried in the direction of the smoke. Soon, I was standing at the door of a sturdily-built cabin, strikingly different from the huts of Periche. The door of the cabin was open just a crack, and sensing I was welcome, I opened it all the way.

Instantly, my eyes were drawn to a blazing fire that crackled in a giant hearth. A large, indistinguishable figure—I couldn't see his face— stood kindly in the shadows beside the hearth. No words passed between us. There was only the great, wonderful presence of his love. I had never been here before. I was home. I was home at last.

I awakened the next morning deeply conflicted. On the one hand, I felt encouraged by the dream and the cabin filled with light. On the other, I felt anxious, confused and still in the dark about all that "accepting Jesus" would entail. Now that I'm "a Christian" would I have to shout "Hallelujah!" or "Praise the Lord!" every time something good or encouraging happened? Had I said yes to a life of freedom, or a life of mindless conformity?

Still lying in bed, I directed my doubts heavenward. *If you're really there, God*, I prayed, *I need you to speak to me. Please, God. Speak to me!*

Without thinking, I reached for my Bible on the nightstand beside my bed. I opened it, let the pages settle, and focused on a paragraph near the top of the left-hand page.

> You therefore, my son, be strong with the strength Jesus gives you. Endure hardship as a good soldier of Christ Jesus, and as Christ's soldier do not let yourself become entangled in worldly affairs, for then you cannot please the one who enlisted you in his army. Follow the Lord's rules for doing his work, just as an athlete either follows the rules or is disqualified and wins no prize... Consider what I say, for the Lord will give you understanding in all things. (2 Timothy 2:1-7)

I was astounded. *It was as if God himself was speaking to me*! And his counsel could not have been more clear: *endure hardship…don't get entangled in worldly affairs…play by the rules*. I felt like an army recruit in boot camp. And, in addition to this counsel, he gave me a final encouraging promise: "Consider what I say, and I will give you understanding in all things." *How cool is that!*

I still had my doubts, of course. But the dream—and the biblical exhortation that followed—were just what I needed to stay on track.

✳✳✳

At the urging of my new Christian friends, I decided to move from Long Island to Brooklyn. Since the Shepherd's House was full at the moment, I was invited to live at another communal house in Brooklyn near Fort Greene Park. It was simply called "The Oxford Street House."

I vividly recall walking for the first time to Oxford Street. *I can't believe I'm doing this*, I marveled, as I hiked passed dingy stoops and littered alleyways. *How did I end up here?*

Just then I noticed a metal sign on the opposite side of the street. "Brooklyn Hospital" it read.

I stopped dead in my tracks. Unbelievable! I gasped. Frank and I were *born* in that building!

The irony did not escape me. After more than four years traipsing the globe, I had been brought back within walking distance of my birthplace!

"Let's try this one more time," God seemed to be saying to me as I gaped at the sign across the street.

"Sure," I replied inwardly. "I'm all in."

Chapter Twenty One

ONCE AT OXFORD STREET, I QUICKLY embraced the lifestyle adhered to by all house residents. With more than 30 people living at Oxford Street, house rules included pooling incomes; rising before dawn for devotions; and attending biweekly Bible studies. I didn't realize it at the time, but it was just the kind of 24/7 structure I needed.

As members of a California-based "denomination" called Gospel Outreach (GO), the Oxford Street residents, along with those at Shepherd's House, had moved to New York to serve among the poor and share the Good News of Jesus Christ. As a "baby Christian," I had only a modest understanding of this Good News. But I clung to the promise that I believed God had given me—that over time he would "give me understanding in all things..."

My first order of business was to find a job. Responding to an ad in *The New York Times*, I interviewed for a job as a copy editor at the prestigious New York publishing house, Simon & Shuster.

"What were you doing between 1970 and 1974?" the person who interviewed me asked, intrigued by the four-year gap in my resume.

"I, ah, well...I guess you could say I was accumulating experiences," I replied.

Needless to say, I did not get the job. In fact, I had a hard time finding work of any kind. Finally, eager to carry my weight at Oxford Street, I took a job as a "rough carpenter" at Todd's Shipyard in Red Hook. I soon discovered that the word "rough" had more than one meaning.

At Todd's, rough carpenters were responsible for repairing the dry docks, work that entailed cutting out damaged sections of the docks and replacing them with new, 12" X 12" timbers. It was as far from finished carpentry as one could get, and required the daily use of chainsaws, oversized drills, and ten-pound sledge hammers.

But the word "rough" also applied to the working conditions at Todd's. Unlike the shipyard's band-saw operators and machinists, rough carpenters spent most of their time outdoors, and by early November— when the first snows came— hammering 18" bolts into solid oak timbers morphed our work crew into a Siberian chain gang.

To make matters worse, I was one of five Oxford Street residents then working at the shipyard. And with big black crosses painted on our hard hats, we were not shy about sharing our faith. Not surprisingly, this did not sit well with all of Todd's workers. On one occasion, in fact, while we were worshipping in the shipyard showers, an unseen critic applauded our efforts by tossing in a large stack of firecrackers. Never in the history of showering had singers turned more quickly into dancers.

But challenges at work were often compensated for by words of encouragement at home. And, for me at least, such words came most frequently from Tommy Kennedy, the red-bearded Scotsman. As the "presiding elder" of GO's work in Brooklyn, Tommy was the one who typically addressed the Oxford Street and Shepherd's House residents—along with other members of our fellowship who did not live communally—when we gathered on Sundays at a meeting hall in Flatbush.

"I've entitled my message this morning, 'No Accidents in the Heart of God,'" Tommy began one of his most memorable Sunday sermons. "Please open your Bibles to Psalm 139.

"Joseph, would you please read out loud verses thirteen through sixteen?" It was not unusual for Tommy, a firm believer in group participation, to ask a member of the congregation to read aloud from the Scriptures.

I stood up, turned to Psalm 139, and began to read.

For you created my inmost being;

You knit me together in my mother's womb...

When I was woven together in the depths of the earth,

Your eyes saw my unformed body...

All the days ordained for me

Were written in your book

Before one of them came to be.

What amazing statements, I remember thinking.

"Thank you, Joseph," Tommy said. "And now, please turn to the first chapter of Ephesians, verses three through five. Joseph, please read aloud for us again."

I turned to Ephesians.

Blessed be the God and Father of our Lord Jesus Christ, who has

blessed us with every spiritual blessing in the heavenly places in Christ,

just as He chose us in Him before the foundation of the world to become,

in Christ, his holy blameless children.

"And finally," Tommy piped, "drop down to the second chapter of Ephesians, verse ten, and read that as well, Joseph."

For we are God's workmanship, created in Christ Jesus for good

works, which God prepared in advance for us to do.

There was a long pause as Tommy tweaked the tip of his moustache and scanned the congregation.

"Brothers and sisters," he then proclaimed, his Scottish brogue adding authority to his words. "*We are no accidents!* God chose us in him before the world was made! We are *His* workmanship, created by Him for good works, which He has already prepared for us to do!

"Brothers and sisters, we are no accidents," he repeated. "We are here—every one of us—for a purpose. And if we press on, we will fulfill that purpose, and God will be glorified."

For more than an hour Tommy hammered this point home. It reminded me of my work at Todd's—every scripture, every story, every inflection in Tommy's voice like the slow, steady pounding of a sledgehammer.

That night, as I lay awake in the brother's dorm at Oxford Street, I reflected back on Tommy's message. Closing my eyes, I pictured God "knitting" Frank and me together in our mother's womb. I pictured him weaving with great care the sinews in our legs, the chambers of our hearts, the lashes on each of our eyes.

"We're no accident!" Tommy's words reverberated in the back of my head. "No accident…no accident…no accident…"

And then I had an unexpected thought.

Had God made me smaller than Frank for a reason?

As far back as I could remember, I had thought of my size compared to Frank's as a kind of curse, a handicap, a burden to be borne. But what if God had made me smaller for a reason, for some pre-ordained purpose I could not yet fully comprehend? The thought appealed to me; but it was something I still struggled to believe. Perhaps I will someday, I mused, as I drifted off to sleep in the darkness of the Oxford Street brother's dorm. Perhaps someday I will.

Chapter Twenty Two

BY NOW, I HAD SPENT NINE months at Oxford Street, adhering to the daily regimen and "enduring hardship as a good soldier of Christ Jesus." But my patience was wearing thin. It had been snowing the past two days, and work at the shipyard was even harder than normal. How I longed to join the other dockhands who warmed themselves beside blazing oil drums. But this was not an option for the carpenters from Oxford Street. We were disciples of Jesus! Servants of the Most High God! Obedient to our masters, as unto the Lord!

But with each passing day, as I rose before dawn and slouched home after dark, the strain and monotony of my life in Brooklyn began to take its toll. Now, after two days of laboring in snow, I returned to Oxford Street on the brink of a breakdown. Weary and confused, I climbed the three flights of stairs that led to the Oxford Street prayer room—a square, high-ceilinged room furnished only with oversized pillows—closed the door behind me, and began to cry.

"I can't live like this anymore, God!" I wept, as I threw myself on one of the prayer room pillows. "I can't! I can't! I can't!"

I had been whining like this for no more than a minute when suddenly a strange and unexpected presence entered the room. *Is that you, Lord?* I wondered. I then felt a pressure on my back, as if a thick woolen blanket had been placed across my shoulders.

"I love you, Joseph," I heard someone say, not audibly, but as plain as day. "I love you…I love you…I love you…"

The tears flowed more freely now. And while the pain in my heart persisted, I was now comforted by those three balm-like words—"I love you"…"I love you"—that pulsated in the prayer room like a beating heart.

"And my will for your life, Joseph," the inaudible voice continued, "is that you be a servant."

I began to cry harder now.

A servant? I protested. *How can that be?! Don't you know who I am, God? I'm the son of a U.S. Congressman! A graduate of Rutgers College! A world-traveling seeker of truth! There must be some mistake!*

I did not actually say these words, of course. But this was how I felt. Surely, God had a better, higher, more illustrious calling on my life than *servant!*

Then, like a foul-tasting pill encased in a spoonful of sugar, the final addendum of the message slid grimly down the throat of my consciousness.

And this will ALWAYS be my will for you, Joseph. And I love you...I love you...I love you...

Then, as quickly as it had appeared, the blanket lifted from my shoulders, and I was alone again, tearful and undone, on the floor of the empty prayer room.

Sitting up, I was flooded by a surge of conflicting emotions. On the one hand, I was disappointed. A servant? *For the rest of my life?* It was a destiny that seemed too daunting, too incomprehensible, too... well, unattractive...to be embraced, and it loomed before me like a bottomless pit.[17]

But more powerful than my feelings of disappointment were my feelings of inexplicable peace. It was as if a tiny sponge, deep inside my soul, had been moistened for the very first time. I now knew—in a way I had never known or believed before—that the God of the Bible... the living, personal God of the universe...not only existed, but he loved me...LOVED me... loved *ME!*

---

17. I would soon realize that serving Jesus Christ would lead me toward the greatest and most rewarding adventures of my life.

Chapter Twenty Three

IT DID NOT TAKE LONG FOR my confidence in God's love to be put
to the test. Less than a month after my experience in the prayer room,
I was approached by another Gospel Outreach elder in Brooklyn, Dave
Sczepanski. A boyish-looking man with straight blond hair and wire-
rimmed glasses, Dave was then in direct spiritual authority over my life.

"There's something we would like you to pray about, Joe," he informed
me, after one of our biweekly Bible studies. "A new GO church has started
upstate, in a small college town called Oswego. We think you'd be an asset
up there, Joe. We'd like you to consider joining them."

I was stunned. I still had fond memories of the Adirondacks, but living
in upstate New York was not what I'd envisioned for my life. I'd been
hoping, in fact, to join one of GO's church-planting teams to Europe or
Central America. But Oswego? I'd never even heard of the place.

Dave went on to explain that the new Oswego church had been
founded by an anthropology professor and former Christian missionary
named Paul Wagner. Apparently, Paul had drifted from the faith after
serving two years in Brazil as a Wycliffe Bible Translator. Soon after
returning to the States, he took a job as an anthropology professor at
Oswego State, a branch of the State University of New York. As part
of his research for a doctoral thesis on the 1970s Jesus Movement,
Paul had journeyed to California where he visited the headquarters of
Gospel Outreach, a former Coast Guard station near Eureka called the
Lighthouse Ranch. There, impressed by the zeal and commitment of the
GO believers, Paul rededicated his life to Christ. He returned to Oswego
boldly proclaiming his resurgent faith. Soon, more than thirty Oswego
State students were attending Saturday night Bible studies at Paul's ranch-
style home on the outskirts of town. Overwhelmed by the growth, Paul
contacted Eureka requesting assistance. With several men and women from

GO churches on the West Coast already on their way, I was now being asked to join them.

"We think you'd be a strong addition, Joe," Dave insisted. "Why don't you pray about it? Then let us know what you think."

After several days praying, I decided to go for it. Oswego was not a place I would have ever chosen to live. But I was traveling on someone else's tracks now. And where he was taking me was where I wanted, or at least was willing, to go.

✳✳✳

I arrived in Oswego in the middle of the biggest snowstorm I had ever seen in my life. Situated on the shores of Lake Ontario, Oswego was famous for its "lake-effect" blizzards, and proud of its record for the second-heaviest snowfall in U.S. history (after Lake Tahoe). On the evening of my arrival, a Bible study was underway in Paul's living room, and more than thirty college students, bright-eyed and bushy-tailed, were jammed into every available space. Though barely 26, I suddenly felt like a senior citizen. *What am I doing here?* I wondered, as I took a seat beside the fireplace.

I was thinking this when suddenly a fresh-faced boy with perfect blond hair began strumming his guitar.

"It only takes a spark to get a fire going. And soon all those around can feel the fire glowing." Within seconds, every kid in the room was swaying from side to side and singing at the top of his lungs. If I felt like a misfit before, I felt like a Martian now.

What on earth am I doing here? I wondered again as the last vestiges of my world-wise persona clung to me like filthy rags.

After five or six songs, Paul rose to his feet to open the meeting with prayer and to make some announcements. Well over six feet tall, with a barrel-chest, neatly-trimmed goatee, and booming voice, Paul cut an imposing figure.

It was no wonder that he commanded the respect of everyone in the room. The announcements over, Paul turned suddenly in my direction.

"And now I'd like to introduce the newest member of our fellowship," he smiled. "His name is Joe Anfuso, and he's come all the way from Brooklyn to be part of what God is doing in Oswego. Is there anything you'd like to share with us, Joe?"

"Well, I uh…I'm really glad to be here," I lied, standing to my feet. "I look forward to all God has in store for us in the days ahead. I'm sure it's going to be a rich and exciting journey."

I wonder if anyone could tell I was lying, I thought, as I re-took my seat.

Paul then launched into a forty-minute sermon that put his keen intellect and superior speaking skills on vivid display. It was self-deprecating, insightful and laced with humor. I was impressed.

At the end of his message, Paul placed a folding metal chair in the center of the room, and asked if anyone needed prayer.

Nearly a minute passed before a girl with long brown hair and green eyes suddenly emerged from the back of the room. She had apparently arrived late and taken a seat on the floor out of my line of vision. She was someone I would have noticed.

"So, how can we pray for you, Karen?" Paul asked as the girl settled shyly into the folding chair. She seemed older than the college kids in the room; something I later learned was true.

"Well, as many of you know, I'm just coming off a serious relationship," she began with disarming candor. "I know it's a good thing. And now I just want God's will. I know his grace is sufficient, but I also need the strength and support of my Christian family. I'd appreciate it if you'd pray for me."

I felt an immediate attraction to this girl, as if our spirits vibrated on the same frequency. She was also stunningly beautiful.

Maybe Oswego won't be so bad after all, I thought, as I gathered with the others around Karen to pray.

KAREN BRENNAN, CIRCA 1975.

Chapter Twenty Four

IT WAS MONTHS BEFORE THE TIME seemed right to pursue a relationship with Karen. She needed time to focus on her relationship with God, and I was busy starting a vinyl-repair business (we fixed car seats), sharing my faith with students at Oswego State, and leading worship at our fledgling church. It was nearly four months, in fact, before I initiated our first real conversation.

The occasion was a potluck at Paul's. It was early May, and the snow had finally melted. As usual, Paul's house was crammed with students all eagerly anticipating the start of summer break. Karen was there, too, wearing leather boots, blue jeans, and a hunter-green blouse that matched her eyes.

"I, ah...I thought you might like to go for a walk?" I asked her, as soon as she'd finished eating.

She seemed surprised. I thought my heart would burst through my T-shirt.

"Why, sure," she finally said. "It sure is a beautiful day."

Soon we were strolling down a quiet country lane lined with tall oak and elm trees that rose majestically against a cloudless sky. The only thing I knew about Karen at that point was that her last name was Brennan; she drove a Volkswagen bug; and that she worked as an administrative assistant at Niagara Mohawk, the local power company. Anxious to know more, I peppered her with questions.

Where were you born? How many brothers and sisters do you have? What does your dad do for a living?

In less than thirty minutes, I learned that she had been born in a small town north of New York City called Central Valley. She was the third of nine children (nine!), all with traditional Irish names: Kevin, Maureen, Terrance, and so on. And that her dad was a small-town attorney, the only one of four brothers to leave the farm. I learned, too, that she had surrendered her life to Christ two years earlier at a Billy Graham movie called *A Time to Run.*

"At the end of the film I thought everyone in the theater would go forward," she smiled, an impish twinkle in her eye. "But I was the only one."

There was something refreshingly unpretentious about this girl, I thought as she spoke. I liked her. I liked her a lot.

And then it was my turn. On and on I rambled, telling her about my childhood in Brooklyn, my relationships with Dad and Frank, my college years, and the travels that followed. Karen listened politely, though I noticed a surprising disinterest in my exotic, post-college adventures. For the first time in my life, it seemed, a woman seemed interested in me— the *real* me—behind all the insecure boasting and bravado. I was captivated.

We had been talking for what seemed like seconds when suddenly a street lamp blinked on above our heads.

"I guess we should head back to Paul's," Karen smiled. As we strolled together side by side in the balmy New York dusk, it suddenly seemed that winter was over not only in Oswego, but in some deep and lonely corner of my heart.

✳✳✳

In the days and weeks that followed I would spend more and more time with Karen. We took long walks, read the Bible together, and, on weekends, frequented "The Loop," a popular fish and hamburger stand on the shores of Lake Ontario. Initially, I was guarded, hinting to Karen that Jesus came first in my life, that he always would, and that I was committed, first and foremost, to pursuing his plan for my life.

It wasn't long, though, before my caution gave way to confidence, and I was confiding in her the deep and hidden secrets of my heart. I shared my fears, my doubts, my insecurities. I told her about Frank and the struggles I had had as his twin.

"You've got so much going for you, Joseph," I remember her telling me on one occasion. "You don't need to compare yourself with anyone."

It was good advice, of course. And I seemed to be having some success in that regard. That is, until I received a mid-July phone call from Frank.

Like hundreds of other Christians that summer, Frank was on his way to Canada to join in a large evangelistic outreach at the 1976 Summer Olympics in Montreal. It had been nearly three years since I'd seen him.

"Hey, Joe, I'm driving through upstate New York this week, and I'd like to stop by and see you. Maybe I can even speak at one of your church services!"

"Sure," I said, my stomach suddenly twisting into knots. "That'd be great. I'll see if I can make some arrangements."

I spoke with Paul, who'd already heard of Francis, and a special midweek meeting was called. Frank—who now preferred to be called Francis—had been gaining a reputation as a gifted speaker and evangelist.

The meeting was held shortly after Francis' arrival at "The Lord's House," a big, white Victorian near the Oswego State campus where I'd been living with fifteen other GO church members. As was our custom, we met in the dining room, a large, high-ceilinged room with dark mahogany paneling and white lace curtains. Frank and I had barely had a chance to speak when Paul called the meeting to order.

"We're pleased to have a special guest with us tonight," Paul began. "Joe's twin brother, Francis! He's come all the way from California to share the word of God with us. Let's give him a warm welcome."

A wave of electricity vibrated through the room as Frank stood in response to a brief round of applause. Dressed in blue jeans and a grey flannel shirt, he seemed accustomed to such greetings, and his eyes glowed with confidence.

After only one or two worship songs, Frank was given the floor to speak. I sat upright in my chair and braced myself. Was he as gifted a speaker as I had heard?

"Beloved, you and I have the awesome privilege of being ambassadors for Christ," he began, his voice charged with emotion. *Is everyone wondering why Frank and I look so different,* I fretted, just I had done for decades.

For nearly an hour, Frank had everyone in the palm of his hand. He was funny, poignant, enthusiastic, convincing. He was, in short, brilliant.

What are Karen and the others thinking? I continued to fret. *Are they wondering why I'm not as gifted... as animated... as charged with emotion as Frank? Is Karen more attracted to Frank than she is to me?*

Before the meeting was over, just as Frank was inviting people to come forward for prayer, I slipped from the dining room and fled to my bedroom upstairs. I closed the door behind me and lay down quietly on my bed. With my hands clasped behind my head and my eyes fixed blankly at the ceiling, I found myself drowning in a pool of self-pity.

What the hell is wrong with me? I muttered. *I thought I was over all this stuff. Won't I ever get over this stuff?*

Just then, I heard Karen calling me from the bottom of the stairs. "Joseph... Joseph." I did not answer. I did not leave my room, in fact, until morning.

The next afternoon, I drove with Karen to one of our favorite hangouts: a small clump of Dogwood trees just up from the lake. It was nearly sunset, and the sky was a purplish pink.

"Where'd you go last night?" Karen asked as the sun slipped slowly toward the horizon. "I couldn't find you after the meeting."

"Oh, I was tired," I said matter-of-factly. "I'd had a hard day at work and went straight to bed."

"Really?" she persisted. "You looked wide awake to me."

I ignored her. Several seconds passed as I sat silently staring at the sinking sun.

"So, what did you think of Francis?" I finally asked, feigning indifference. "He's a good speaker, huh?"

A knowing smile now spread across Karen's face.

"So, *that's* what it was," she laughed, her green eyes flashing. "I thought so. Why, Joseph Anfuso, you're pathetic do you know that? Why do you insist on comparing yourself with other people? Sure, he's a good speaker. But so what? You're every bit as special as he is, Joseph… don't you see that?"

I was stunned by her frankness. How had she known what I was feeling?

"But…" I started to defend myself.

"Oh, forget your buts," she cut me off. "Look, just this morning I read something in the Book of Galatians."

She reached into her purse and pulled out the pocket New Testament I'd recently given her, opened it and began to read. "If anyone thinks he is something when he is nothing, he deceives himself. Each one should test his own actions. Then he can take pride in himself, without comparing himself to somebody else, for each one should carry his own load." (Galatians 6:3-5)

She closed the Bible quickly and locked me in a steady gaze.

"Joseph, you've got more going for you than you realize," she said, impatiently. "Why don't you just be yourself?"

I was getting a little frustrated now. *Who did she think she was lecturing...*

"And besides," she said, before I could say anything, "*I* like you just the way you are."

I opened my mouth to speak, but could not. It was as if God himself was speaking to me, telling me again through Karen that he loved me, approved of me, wanted to use me. Not like Frank, or anyone else for that matter. Like *Joseph*...like the flawed but useful person he had made me.

Without a word, I slid my arm around Karen's waist and pulled her gently to my side. By now, the sun was a deep vermillion, more beautiful than I had ever seen it. I recalled the many sunsets I had seen in Oswego in recent months, and how I had neutralized their beauty, comparing them to sunsets in Hawaii, India or Greece. But now I could see only the wonder of God's creation, the obedient sun quietly declaring the glory of its Maker.

A prayer formed slowly, silently in my heart. *O, God, make me to shine someday for your glory. Help me, Lord, to be the person* YOU *made me to be.*

Chapter Twenty Five

FROM THAT DAY FORWARD, I DEVOTED myself to whatever
opportunities God gave me to serve. I reached out to people who
struggled with feelings of inadequacy, condemnation or self-hatred. I
wrote worship songs, some of which became standards at our weekly
church services. And I launched a quarterly newsletter, *The Oswego
Oracle*, which I faithfully mailed to other GO churches, in the U.S. and
overseas. In each endeavor, I sought to embrace the following principles.

First, I determined to start where I was, with what I had. "Do not
despise the day of small beginnings," (Zechariah 4:10) the Bible advised
me, and I took the exhortation to heart.

Second, I rejected the pressure, present in my life since childhood,
to be "the best" at what I did. It no longer mattered if I was "better" or
"worse" than someone else. All that mattered was that I used whatever
gifts God had given me to the best of *my* ability.

And finally, I refused to assess the value of my God-assigned tasks.
If God gave me something to do, it had value. And neither I nor anyone
else could put a price tag on its worth.

One thing I *did* put a price tag on, though, was my deepening
relationship with Karen. It was priceless. Her pure, constant love was
a picture to me of God's love. And as the weeks and months rolled by
I was increasingly aware that of all the gifts I'd ever been given, Karen
was the best. I would ask her to marry me on a one-day outing to nearby
Niagara Falls. "It's about time!" she laughed as soon as I'd popped the
question. Like most women, she knew what was happening long before
me.

With marriage on the horizon, and the need for new digs
increasingly apparent, I began to search for a suitable apartment. Before
long, mutual friends and longtime residents of Oswego offered us the

second floor of a lovely, turn-of-the-century townhouse. It had two baths, a veranda, and a large formal dining room with built-in cabinets and French doors. Karen loved it.

Everything was pointing toward settling in Oswego when I received an unexpected letter from Dave Sczepanski. He was back in California now, having just assumed leadership of GO's media ministry, Radiance.

Why is Dave writing me? I wondered as I tore into the envelope.

"I've been reading with interest your well-done newsletter from Oswego," the letter began. "Right now we have a need at Radiance for someone to help with our publications. Would you be willing to pray about coming to Eureka…"

The words seemed to leap from the page. California! Writing! A job I might actually *love!* After two years fixing vinyl, and a year at Todd's Shipyard before that, Dave's letter impacted me like a pardon from the Governor's office. And since I'd done nothing to seek Dave's invitation and had been willing to stay on in Oswego, I was convinced that California was the next step in God's plan for my life. I was ecstatic.

Karen, too, was excited. She loved upstate New York and would miss her family, but images of palm trees and sandy beaches glimmered in her imagination.

Our wedding took place on February 26, 1977—during one of the biggest blizzards either of us had ever seen. Paul Wagner and Tommy Kennedy officiated, and Frank and Victor served as my best men. Karen looked stunning, of course, in a simple white gown covered with eyelet, and holding a red long-stemmed rose. I'd even written a song for the occasion, which I sang to her as she walked down the aisle.

"Come, my sister, my friend…we will enter in…we will live for him…we will tell of the wonders of his love…"

Not the most romantic of tunes, but one that reflected our deepening devotion to Christ and his calling on our lives.

As Karen and I drove west from Oswego, with everything we owned shoehorned into her Volkswagen Bug, our hearts brimmed with love and anticipation. We would spend the next four weeks chugging across America, from the Blue Ridge Mountains of Virginia, through the South and Southwest, and finally up the California coastline to Eureka. The first chapter of our life together had begun, and we embraced it with hope, optimism and unbridled joy.

KAREN AND I SHORTLY AFTER OUR ARRIVAL IN
CALIFORNIA IN 1977.

Chapter Twenty Six

SOON AFTER OUR ARRIVAL IN EUREKA, Karen and I settled into a small second-floor apartment in the heart of town, Unfortunately, Eureka was not the "California" Karen had envisioned—redwoods and constant fog versus palm trees and constant sunshine. But her disappointment was mitigated by the sheer excitement of having our own place. With very little money at our disposal, we filled our apartment with secondhand furniture, including a large wooden spool, compliments of the local phone company, which served as our dining room table. We were disoriented, impoverished, uncertain of the future, but happy as clams.

Eager to hone my writing skills, I took a job at the *Tri-City Weekly*, a local advertising shopper then owned and managed by Gospel Outreach. In addition to classified ads, each issue featured two or three local-interest stories, a part of the paper for which I was responsible. Every week I scoured the town for anything newsworthy, writing stories on the Coast Guard, company-owned logging towns, stout commercial fishermen and septuagenarian apple growers. It was more fun than I'd had in ages, and I loved it.

In addition to writing for the *Tri-City Weekly*, I took on part-time assignments for Radiance, GO's media ministry. At first, I converted sermons by GO's founder, Jim Durkin, into articles for the ministry's monthly periodical, *Radiance Magazine*. By now, there were more than 60 GO churches in the U.S., as well as small but growing congregations in Germany, England, Italy and Guatemala. It wasn't long before Dave and I began ghostwriting books for Jim, two of which—*Living the Word* and *Life with a Purpose*—were published by a small Christian publishing house in Ann Arbor, Michigan, Servant Books.

Anxious to find a broader audience for Jim's books, Dave asked me to attend a writer's conference in Portland, Oregon, eight hours drive north of Eureka. Editors from several Christian publishing houses would be gathering for the conference. It would be an ideal place to make some contacts, and I was happy to oblige.

The venue was Warner Pacific College, a small evangelical university in the center of town. Nearly one thousand people attended that year—from fledgling writers like myself to published authors with multiple titles under their belts. When I arrived on the Warner Pacific campus, my emotions ranged from fervor to flat-out intimidation.

In addition to attending workshops—most aimed at helping people get into print—I busied myself trying to make appointments with Christian publishers. I was thrilled when Virginia Muir, the Managing Editor of Tyndale House Publishers, agreed to meet with me.

A distinguished-looking, seventy-something lady with gray hair pulled up in a bun, Mrs. Muir had an air of benevolent authority about her. She listened intently as I sat with her in the Warner Pacific lobby. I had barely finished extolling the merits of Jim's teaching, when she asked me a totally unexpected question.

"So, tell me about yourself, Joseph," she said. "How did you come to know Jesus?"

I was stunned. Why would an editor from a leading Christian publishing house want to know about me? I'd been a Christian for only three years, and what little I knew about theology and God's Word I had picked up from others. *She's just being polite*, I assumed.

Not wanting to be rude, I spent the next five or ten minutes fumbling through a thumbnail sketch of my testimony. Mrs. Muir listened quietly, her hands folded matronly in her lap, and her eyes filled with kindness.

"Thank you for sharing with me, Joseph," she said when I was finished. "I enjoyed meeting you."

She then rose to her feet, shook my hand, and went quickly on her way. *Nice lady,* I thought, as I watched her disappear into the crowd.

Two weeks later, I received a letter on Tyndale House letterhead.

Dear Joseph,

It was a pleasure to meet you at the Warner Pacific Writer's Conference. I'm sorry we didn't have more time to talk, but I could tell by just the short conversation we had that you have a wonderful story to tell.

I don't always encourage writers to record their personal experiences, but in your case I feel it would be well worthwhile for you to outline an autobiographical story concerning your struggles with eastern religions and, of course, the most important part of your story would be the fact that you found the Lord Jesus.

God bless you in your newspaper work. I will look forward to hearing from you.

Virginia J. Muir

Managing Editor

Tyndale House Publishers

I was flabbergasted. I glanced at the top of the page to re-check the letterhead. Looks real to me, I thought. *But how can this be?* We had spoken for barely twenty minutes, and half of that time had been devoted to talking about Jim. Did she really think my story was "wonderful"?

It would take me five weeks to cobble together the "autobiographical outline" Mrs. Muir had requested. Finally—like a gambler slipping a coin into a one-armed bandit—I dropped the outline into the "Out of Town" slot at the Eureka post office. All I could do now was wait.

Three weeks later, I received another letter.

> Dear Joseph,
>
> The outline is fascinating. I read it through very carefully and am now going to pass it along to Dr. Hawley who is our Editor-in-Chief….It's a touching and thrilling story, Joseph, and I'm happy you shared it with me.

Yahoo! I whooped inwardly. *I can't believe it. Is this possible? Am I really going to be* a published author?

Well, not exactly. Two weeks and nine days later, I received a third letter from Tyndale House.

> Dear Joseph,
>
> I have examined your fascinating and promising material for a potential book and must regretfully inform you that it lies outside the publishing needs of Tyndale House at this time.
>
> Therefore, I heartily suggest that you continue your search for a publisher who will enthusiastically publish your material. And, once again, we thank you for thinking of Tyndale House.

The letter, dated March 7, 1979, was signed: "Wendell Hawley, Editor in Chief." Naturally, I was crestfallen. But, encouraged by Mrs. Muir, I sent my outline to Peter Gilquist, then an editor at Thomas Nelson Publishers.

"It is my opinion that you have the framework for a book," Mr. Gilquist replied. "However, I am declining the opportunity to pursue this project with you, and suggest that you take it to Roy Carlisle at Harper & Row."

Which I did. Several weeks later, Mr. Carlisle wrote me this: "In one of those rare moments of quietness I picked up your story and spent considerable time perusing it….Unfortunately, it is not something we would be inclined to publish….Also, it is very hard to judge this type of proposal because it is not the actual writing but a synopsis-like presentation. I would either do one or the other. The synopsis should be shorter or you should actually write the manuscript."

But the most discouraging feedback from Mr. Carlisle came during my follow-up phone call to him. "Joe, this seems like something you'd write when you're much older," he told me. "You know, when you're in your fifties."

My fifties! Wouldn't the Second Coming have taken place by then?

I simply couldn't wait that long. So, I took Mr. Carlisle's advice and wrote a manuscript. It would take me two years. At last, bolstered by Karen's support and extraordinary typing skills, I simultaneously submitted the manuscript to Bridge Publishing in New Jersey, and Victor Books in Wheaton, Illinois. Their response? Two more rejection slips; although each offered a glimmer of hope: "We find your manuscript interesting and well written" (Victor); "Without a doubt, you will be able to find a publisher" (Bridge).

Not ready to throw in the towel, I decided to make one last submission to Chosen Books in Lincoln, Virginia. Renowned for their personal experience narratives—*The Hiding Place* by Corrie ten Boom and *Born Again* by Charles Colson, for example—Chosen was a highly-respected firm with a long track record of success. And so—reminding myself that even the world's greatest writers receive rejection slips—I clung to my dream of a published book.

Several weeks passed. Finally, just when I thought my dream was dead, I received a phone call from Chosen's Editorial Manager, Dave Hazard.

"I'd like to work with you on your project, Joe," he said. "You're going to have to re-write your manuscript, though. And I can't guarantee Chosen will ever publish it. But if you're willing to work with us, we're willing to work with you."

I felt like post-resurrection Lazarus. It wasn't a contract, but it wasn't a rejection either!

Maybe my persistence is paying off! I gloated. I had no idea, however, that the "pay off" would be far different—and far greater—than anything I could have imagined.

Chapter Twenty Seven

As it turned out, my project with Chosen was not the only manuscript I would have to write from scratch. Recently, a member of GO's church in Guatemala, Efrain Rios Montt, had become the president of that country, and Dave Sczepanski and I decided to tell his story. Thomas Nelson agreed to publish the book under the title, *The New Guatemala*, and with TV personality Pat Robertson on board to write the foreword, it seemed like a project destined for success.

To write the book, Dave and I would have to make several trips to Guatemala, a beautiful Central American country with a history of violence and political unrest. It was during one of these visits, in the spring of 1982, that I decided to visit GO's missionary in Nicaragua, Bob Trolese. I remember deplaning at the airport in Managua and passing nervously through customs. The Sandinistas were in power at the time, and the terminal was crawling with grim-faced soldiers toting AK-47s.

Where's Bob? I remember fretting, as I stood in the dark outside the terminal. At last, Bob pulled up in a small red pickup truck heavily laden with what appeared to be sacks of rice. A mild-mannered man with an infectious smile, Bob greeted me with a hug.

"Welcome to Nicaragua, Joe," he smiled, as he wedged my suitcase between two sacks of grain. "It's great to see you."

I would spend the following day with Bob, visiting the orphanage he had started for local street kids, and two schools the Sandinista Government had entrusted into his care.

"They're *Christian* schools now," he said with obvious satisfaction. "They don't care what we do at the schools, as long as we run them."

At the end of the day, Bob took me on a tour of his offices, a maze of narrow hallways and cave-like rooms. I was walking down one of the hallways when I noticed a wood-mounted poster hanging on one of the nearby walls. For some reason, the image on the poster looked familiar. Stepping closer, I saw that it was a cluster of crude stone huts overshadowed by enormous snow-capped peaks.

I think I know where that is! I gasped inwardly.

Leaning forward, I read the barely-legible script at the bottom of the poster: *Photo by Willi P. Burkhardt. Periche, Himalaya.*

I nearly fell to the floor. *It was Periche...*the Nepalese village I had dreamed about the night I accepted Christ!

I now turned to the scripture verse, written in Spanish, at the top of the poster. "Can you please translate that for me, Bob?" I asked, struggling to keep my composure.

"Sure," he said. "Your righteousness is like the great mountains; your judgments as deep as the canyons, Psalm 36:6."

A series of images—once disconnected—now flashed cohesively through my mind. I saw Frank running at me from the door of Morningstar Ranch...Jerry Russell flagging down our school bus on the outskirts of Sacramento... Sabine sharing her testimony in the prayer circle at Table Mountain...and the tract-distributing Jesus Freaks at the border of Pakistan and India.

How you sought me, Lord, I thought, as I stared at the improbable poster. *Your righteousness is truly like great mountains...your judgments like deep canyons.*

I recounted now to Bob my visit to Periche years earlier, and my dream the night of my conversion.

"For some reason, Bob, this poster reminds me of all the times God intervened in my life, trying to draw me to himself. I don't think I can explain it, but it brings tears to my eyes."

No sooner had I finished than Bob took the poster off the wall and handed it to me.

"This means more to you than it ever will to me," he smiled. "Why don't you take it with you?"

It hangs on the wall above my computer to this day.

✳✳✳

On returning to Guatemala, I decided to visit the church-run school where Rios Montt had been principal prior to becoming president. On the day of the coup that put him in power (you have to read the book), Rios had been standing on the roof of the school watching the jets and helicopters flying low above the city. I wondered what it was like for him on that day.

When I arrived at the school, I ascended at once to the rooftop and stepped toward the waist-high wall that girded its perimeter. Looking out over the city, I visualized jets and helicopters, and tried to imagine what Rios might have been thinking as he watched the unfolding drama. Did he know what was happening? Did he know tanks and howitzers were being rolled into place at the National Plaza, and that soon his name would be broadcast over national radio: "Efrain Rios Montt... report at once to the National Palace!"

I was deep in thought, when suddenly I heard what sounded like the clinking of metal. Lowering my gaze, I saw a small group of young people camping in a nearby courtyard. Two members of the group, a boy and girl in their teens or early twenties, were squatting beside an open spigot cleaning some pots and pans. *I bet they're a mission team from the States,* I surmised. At the time, short-term mission teams were something of a novelty, and I studied the hive of volunteers with rapt attention.

Suddenly, a series of random thoughts jelled into a kind of waking vision. I saw thousands of everyday people leaving the comforts and routine of their lives back home to serve God and others in foreign lands.

That's just what we all need, I thought. More opportunities to put our faith *into action*.

I returned to Eureka convinced that my "vision" in Guatemala was more than a flash-in-the-pan daydream. I still had two manuscripts to write, but the seed of a very different endeavor was now sprouting in my heart.

Eager to share my new vision, I met with one of my good friends at the time, Steve Fish, at a local Chinese restaurant. Between bites of egg rolls and chop suey, I recounted to Steve my experience on the rooftop in Guatemala, my passion to mobilize people for ministry, and my growing conviction that short-term mission teams could be an extraordinarily-effective vehicle for doing that.

"Well…why don't we just *do it?*" Steve said, matter-of-factly, as he cracked open a fortune cookie.

It was all the encouragement I needed. Within days, Steve and I were making plans to start a branch of Gospel Outreach that we decided to call Forward Edge. The name was derived from a sermon by Jim Durkin entitled, "The Forward Edge of Life." As a boy, Jim explained, his mother would cook meals on a wood-burning stove. When she wanted her pots to cool, she moved them to the back edge of the stove. But when she wanted them to heat up, she moved them to the forward edge. "God doesn't want lukewarm followers," Jim insisted. "He wants followers who live, day in and day out, on life's *forward edge!*"[18]

Satisfied that we not only had the right name but the right vehicle,

---

18. Years later, in a discussion with one of our board members at the time, Doug Crane, we would agree on a more current definition of "the forward edge": When God prompts us to do something, and we respond with faith and obedience—even without knowing what lies ahead—we are stepping onto "the forward edge." It is here, on life's forward edge, that we discover in a deeper way who God is, who we are, and what God can do through us.

Steve and I decided to send the first Forward Edge short-term team to Italy where a mutual friend, Andy Costa, was planting a church on the outskirts of Florence. The team was scheduled for October, 1983. I still dreamed of taking a GO church-planting team to Nepal someday, but I was content for now to focus whatever time I could spare on the embryonic ministry of Forward Edge.

✳✳✳

Meanwhile I was chipping away at my autobiographical manuscript for Chosen. Finally, after more than six months of writing, I completed the first seven chapters. I mailed them off to Dave Hazard in Virginia, and arranged to rendezvous with him in a couple weeks at the upcoming Warner Pacific Writer's Conference in Portland. "I'll read the chapters on the plane," he told me. Naturally, I was eager—and not a little anxious—to hear what he thought of them.

We met at The Matterhorn Restaurant not far from the Warner Pacific campus.

"Well, you've read seven chapters now, Dave," I said as I sat across from him in one of the restaurant's booths. "Are you guys going to publish my book?"

There was a pause, and then Dave looked me in the eye and said: "Yes. Congratulations, Joe...you're about to become a published author!"

I was speechless. It seemed too good to be true.

"Are you sure, Dave?" I asked. "I mean, don't you have to take it to a committee of some kind?"

"No...I'm the decision maker now," he said. "I'll send you a contract within two weeks."

I returned to Eureka on cloud nine. Karen was ecstatic, too. At last, my ship had come in!

Within a week, I was checking my mailbox with military precision. Two weeks passed. Then three. No contract. Finally, after more than a month, I decided to call Dave.

"I've been meaning to call, Joe," he said sheepishly. "Chosen has just been purchased by Zondervan. The lines of authority have all changed. But don't worry; just finish the book. There's a 99.9 percent chance you're book will be published."

I hung up the phone and told Karen what had happened. "Oh, don't worry about it, Hon." She smiled, her green eyes sparkling. "Ninety-nine point nine percent sounds pretty good to me. Just do what Dave told you and finish the book. It's a great book, Joe. I'm sure it's going to get published."

Shaken, but hopeful, I spent the next nine months completing the final chapters. I posted them to Dave and waited anxiously for his reply. Point one percent of a hundred was almost too infinitesimal to count… wasn't it?

Chapter Twenty Eight

As the days and weeks rolled past, I tried my best not to obsess about my project with Chosen. I still had the Rios Montt book to write, and I was busy making plans for the first Forward Edge team to Italy. Steve and I had T-shirts made; we compiled pre-trip training materials; and I spent hours on the phone with Andy Costa talking about the team's schedule. It was decided that I should lead the team, which consisted of nine people from various churches around the country. My vision on the Guatemala City rooftop was about to become a reality.

It was about this time that I received an out-of-the-blue phone call from Frank.

"How's it goin', Joe?" he began, a puzzling apprehension in his voice.

"Great," I replied. "I leave for Italy in a couple weeks. And I'm expecting to hear from Chosen any day now about my book."

There was a long pause. Frank knew about my book, of course, as did everyone else in my family, and most of my friends.

"Oh," Frank said.

"Why, what's up, Frank?" I probed.

"Well, I just received a phone call from someone at Zondervan Books. And... well...I guess they've decided not to publish your book. Didn't you know that?"

I was stunned. Why in the world would Frank be informed of this *before me?*

"No, I hadn't heard," I said. A lump began to form in my throat. "Are you sure?"

"Yes, I think so. And..."

There was another long pause.

"And what?" I insisted.

"Well...I guess they want *me* to write a book. I'm sorry, Joe. I thought you knew."

It suddenly felt like an ice pick had been surgically driven into the most private, tender cranny of my heart. I could feel the blood rushing to my cheeks as a tidal wave of emotions overwhelmed me: sadness... jealousy...embarrassment...anger.

"Wow, that's great, Frank," I muttered, barely able to speak. "Really...great. You must be excited."

Another long pause.

"I'm sorry, Joe," Frank repeated. "I thought you knew."

After some awkward goodbyes, I hung up the phone and struggled to process what I had just heard. It had been four years since my encounter with Virginia Muir at Warner Pacific. Four years of writing, re-writing, and starting all over again. Four years of hoping, dreaming, trusting that God was involved in my efforts—and involved not just in my writing, but in my *life*. I knew my trials were tiny compared with those that other people faced. But I was too busy fighting off doubt and self-pity to care about anyone else right now. This was *my* struggle. And it was overwhelming me.

You're a sadist, God, I cried, not audibly, but deep inside my heart... which now was hardening like a block of cement.

I would spend the next several days in mourning. Even Karen could not console me. *How could you be so cruel, God?* I kept hurling accusations heavenward. Wasn't it enough for Zondervan to reject my book? Did they have to ask *Frank* to write a book? You're a sadist, God...a sadist...a sadist...

***

Approximately one month after Frank's phone call, the church in Eureka hosted a GO missionary from Ecuador who purportedly had a powerful gift of prophecy. His name was Jim DeGolyer. Special meetings were called to give Jim ample time to minister. Thinking Jim might be interested in hosting a Forward Edge team someday, Karen and I invited him to our home for dinner.

Having long since vacated our second-floor apartment, Karen and I were now living in a small Tudor-style Craftsman. When Jim arrived, Karen was putting the finishing touches on my favorite meal: curried chicken and saffron rice.

"Come in!" I smiled, as I opened the door to let Jim in. "You're right on time."

Of medium build, with wire-rimmed glasses and a neatly-trimmed beard, he was less intimidating than I'd expected. With dinner ready to be served, I ushered him into our dining room, a cozy nook with leaded glass windows and lace curtains. A missionary in Central America before heading for Ecuador, he was quick to admire our tablecloth, a brightly-embroidered souvenir which I'd purchased for Karen on a recent trip to Guatemala.

During our dinner conversation, I was surprised to learn that Jim and I had some unexpected things in common. A native of upstate New York and a Cornell alum, Jim was intimately familiar with the Adirondacks, and—to my amazement—had even heard of Forest Lake Camp.

"My uncle Ollie used to work there," he said. "Did you know Ollie Van Sise?"

"Of course!" I exclaimed, suddenly aware that he bore a striking resemblance to his uncle. "Ollie was one of our favorite counselors."

I sensed an unexpected kinship with Jim, as if our paths were somehow destined to cross.

After dinner, Jim, Karen and I retired to the living room to continue our conversation. A fire was crackling in the fireplace, and its flames could be seen in the glass of the built-in bookshelves that framed the hearth. We'd been chatting for more than an hour when Jim blurted what seemed at first like a strangely out-of-place question.

"Can I pray for you, Joseph?" he asked, almost in a whisper.

The question took me off guard. *Pray for me?* Why would he want to do that? Had he sensed the recently-formed concrete in my heart?

"Sure," I said, as Karen nodded her approval. "Why not?"

For several minutes, we stood in silence in front of the fireplace as Jim rested his hands gently on my chest.

"Thank you for my brother," he finally prayed. "Thank you for his tender heart and many gifts."

Several more seconds passed.

"Joseph, I'm getting a mental picture of two small babies in a mother's womb. Does that mean anything to you?"

I was startled. *How did he know that?*

"Well...I do have a twin brother," I said.

A smile curled slowly across Jim's face, and his eyes seemed to blanket me with compassion.

"Thank you, Jesus," he prayed, and then closed his eyes.

I closed mine, too, listening with heightened curiosity as the fire seemed to crackle more loudly than before.

"I see a hand with a knife," Jim then said. "The hand is reaching toward a cord in the mother's stomach—not an umbilical cord, but a cord connecting the two babies. The hand is placing the knife against the cord and cutting it. The babies are free now...free to live out their own destinies...to tell their own stories...to fulfill God's plan and purpose for their lives..."

How did he know this? I resisted. *Someone must have told him I have a twin!*

"God is now showing me that for many years you have believed a lie about yourself, Joseph," Jim went on. "The lie is that you are second-rate....And so, in the name of Jesus, I break the power of that lie over your life. Now, and forever more."

Jim then asked me what I was feeling.

"I'm not sure," I said, trying to mask my cynicism. "I appreciate you praying for me, though. I really do. And I'll definitely take what happened here tonight to God in prayer."

Later that night, long after Karen had gone to bed, I was sitting alone on the couch in our living room.

What if Jim's picture was real? I wondered, as I stared at the last glowing embers of the fire. What if God is trying to speak to me through Jim...trying to bestow on me a blessing I'm too proud and too stubborn to receive?

The following night Karen and I attended Jim's first meeting at the GO church. I was a respected leader in our church at the time, an ordained elder, a Bible teacher, and a writer of books. But from the moment I sat down, during the entire worship service and all of Jim's teaching, I found myself filled with self-loathing.

I'm sick of myself, I fumed. *I've been a Christian ten years...but I still feel sorry for myself! When will it end? Is this all there is to being a Christian?*

At last, Jim was done preaching. "Would anyone here like prayer?" he asked.

Without hesitating, I sprung from my seat and walked to the front of the church. *I don't care what others think of me,* I resolved. *I need help!*

Within seconds, I was lying on the floor in the front of the church surrounded by well-meaning friends. I was vaguely aware that they were praying for me, and that the prayers were heartfelt and biblically correct. But I felt no connection to the prayers. I felt only God's presence as three words—words only I could hear—engulfed me like a tidal wave.

I love you, Joseph...I love you...I love you...I love you...

✳✳✳

Two weeks later, I came across a story that clarified for me what had happened during Jim's visit. I stumbled on the story while perusing some planning materials I'd ordered for Forward Edge. The story was told by a man visiting a circus in Tucson, Arizona.

"During one of the breaks at the circus," the man recounted, "I started chatting with the elephant trainer. 'How is it that you can stake down a ten-ton elephant with the same size stake you use for this little fellow? (The 'little fellow' weighed 300 pounds.)

"It's easy when you know two things," the trainer explained. "Elephants really do have good memories, but they aren't very smart. When they're babies, we stake them down. They tug at the stake maybe ten thousand times before they realize they can't break free. At that point, their elephant memory takes over and they remember for the rest of their lives that they can't get away from the stake.

"Humans are sometimes like elephants," the storyteller continued. "When we're young, some unthinking, insensitive, unwise person says 'He's not very smart,' or 'She's not a leader' or 'Your team will never win.' And zap, we drive a mental stake into our minds. Often we become mature adults, and we're still held back by some inaccurate, one-sentence 'stake' put in our minds when we were young."

That's me! I found myself exclaiming as I read the story. And not just me, but countless other people, too. In my case, it had taken Jim identifying "the stake" in my mind ("You're second rate") for me to see what was holding me back. And God—telling me again how much he loved me—for me to finally break free.

I love you, too, I now found myself responding to my heavenly Father with increased frequency and fervor. *I love you, too!*

Chapter Twenty Nine

AND SO, AS IT TURNED OUT, God's blessing was not on my writing, but on my life. Even the Rios Montt book tanked. He was removed from office after just eighteen months, and the very next day an editor from Thomas Nelson called to ask Dave and me to release them from their contract. "May the Lord restore for you the years the locust has eaten," he said, quoting from the Book of Joel. In the end, Dave and I self-published the book under the quasi-humorous title, *He Gives, He Takes Away*. But not surprisingly, few people were interested in reading a book about the ex- president of a country they cared little or nothing about. It would be 25 years before I would try my hand again at serious writing.

But, in his wisdom, God used the failure of my two book projects to do something far greater. *He was setting me free!* "He who the Son sets free," Jesus declared in John 8:36, "is free indeed." Now, ten years after surrendering my life to Christ, I was finally beginning to experience—on a deeper, more personal level—what Jesus meant by the word "indeed."

And not only that, I was learning to view failure, hardships and trials in an entirely new light. "For what son is there who a father does not chasten?" Paul the apostle wrote in Hebrews 12:8. "But if you are without chastening, of which all have become partakers, then you are illegitimate and not a son."

Praise God! I now realized. *I'm A SON!*

I now devoted myself—with renewed confidence in God's unfathomable love—to whatever tasks he set before me. I led the first Forward Edge team to Italy (which turned out to be a great success), and made plans with Steve to send three more teams the following year: one to Guatemala to help build an orphanage; one to Los Angeles for the 1984 Summer Olympics; and one to England to help with a Billy Graham Crusade in Birmingham. I was fulfilling God's plan for my life,

THE FIRST FORWARD EDGE TEAM TO ITALY IN
1983. TEAM MEMBERS ARE INTERSPERSED AMONG
SOME OF OUR ITALIAN CO-WORKERS.

I thought. And it was good.

✳✳✳

All was going well, in fact, when sometime between January and March of 1984 I found myself confronted by an unforeseen dilemma. I could not seem to shake the idea that God might be calling me to Nepal. Church planting, after all, was the primary mission of Gospel Outreach, and since I had lived in Nepal prior to becoming a Christ follower, I wondered if God might want me to plant a church there.

I decided to share my dilemma with GO's founder, Jim Durkin. An ordained Assemblies of God minister, Jim had spent 25 years pastoring a small church in Eureka prior to his involvement with GO. With a congregation that never exceeded 50, Jim had been forced to moonlight as a realtor. I had frequently heard his story about the time two long-haired hippies entered his real estate offices in the summer of 1970.

"Can I help you?" Jim had asked as they stood, wide-eyed and somber, in front of his desk.

"We're looking for a place to hold Bible studies," they told him. "We might even start a coffee shop."

Are these guys Christians? Jim remembered thinking as he scanned their threadbare outfits and shoulder-length hair. His first instinct was to direct them elsewhere. But a verse from the Bible then materialized in his heart: *How does the love of God abide in you if you have it in your power to do good and do it not?*[19]

Convicted by the Holy Spirit, Jim offered the two men a small, unoccupied storefront that was on his list of available properties. He would eventually take the two men and their small band of followers

---

19. *1 John 3:17*

under wing, a decision that would not only change his life, but thousands of others as well. By the spring of 1984, more than 75 GO churches had been planted across the United States, Europe and Latin America. After a quarter of a century pastoring a flock that never reached 50, Jim was now shepherd of a ministry that numbered in the tens of thousands. He was, in short, no stranger to faith, obedience and waiting on God.

That's why I came to Jim with my dilemma. As was his custom with those he counseled, he invited me to join him on a walk. Nearly three hundred pounds and locked in a perpetual battle with his weight, Jim considered walks a way of killing two birds with one stone.

"I'm not sure what to do, Jim," I confided, as we strolled passed an empty storefront in downtown Eureka. "I'm excited about the potential of Forward Edge. But I can't stop wondering if God might be calling me to Nepal."

Jim did not respond at first. He wasn't one to speak glibly when asked for advice.

"Why don't we sit for a minute," he finally said, gesturing toward a nearby bench. "There's a four-sentence story I'd like to tell you. I think it might help."

A four-sentence story?

We sat down, and Jim proceeded to tell me his story:

> A man with a single bucket of water is approaching a building engulfed in flames. Next to the building is a row of sleeping firemen. The man must make a choice. Does he throw his water on the building, or on the row of sleeping firemen?

I sat silent for a moment, pondering the meaning of Jim's riddle. Then, like a magnet sucking up chards of tin, my mind amalgamated a myriad of fragmented thoughts. I had always been drawn, it seemed, to "the little guy"—to those who struggled with feelings of insignificance. I had also sat for years under biblical teaching that emphasized "every-member ministry" over "one-man shows." And, perhaps more than anything, I longed to see this teaching *translated into action.* Now, with the help of Jim's story, I began to realize that God had entrusted me with a vehicle—Forward Edge—that could help thousands of "everyday believers" hear His call on their lives, and respond with faith, obedience, and unflagging devotion.

"Thank you, Jim," I smiled, placing my hand gently on his shoulder. "I think you've helped me solve my dilemma."

THE FORWARD EDGE TO NEPAL IN 1987. I'M
SQUATTING IN THE BACK ROW ON THE LEFT.

MY CHILDREN AROUND THE TIME OF OUR MOVE
TO VANCOUVER, WASHINGTON. FROM LEFT TO
RIGHT: HEATHER, KATELYN AND RYAN.

Chapter Thirty

IN THE MONTHS AND YEARS THAT followed, I watched with wonder as God blessed the ministry of Forward Edge. By 1987, Forward Edge volunteers were building children's homes in Guatemala; ministering to the homeless in New York City; serving among Native Americans in Montana; and treating the sick in Nicaragua. That year, I would even lead a team back to Nepal where we climbed high into the Himalayan Mountains to distribute Nepali translations of the Gospel of John. God had not called me to long-term missionary work, but—through Forward Edge—he was using me to bring his message to the ends of the earth.

In 1989, Karen and I received the blessing of Jim and the GO elders to move from Eureka to the outskirts of Portland, Oregon, where Victor, Kathy and my mother now lived. Mom was suffering from Alzhiemers, and Vic and Kathy needed my help caring for her. There was a GO church in Vancouver, Washington, just across the river from Portland, and since Karen and I were friends of the pastor, as well as others in the congregation, this was where we settled.

We would spend our first eighteen months living in a secluded, 700-square-foot cabin just north of the Vancouver city limits. Over the years, God had blessed Karen and me with three children—Heather, Ryan, and Katelyn—and while the cabin was adequate, it was, to say the least, cramped. Soon, we were able to purchase a two-acre parcel that included a ramshackle barn. With the help of weekend volunteers (many of them veterans of Forward Edge teams), we were able to transform the barn into the new Forward Edge headquarters.

Less than a year after settling in the Northwest, I would take my oldest daughter, Heather, then age 10, on her first Forward Edge mission trip. It was 1990, and the World Cup Soccer Championships or Mondiale was being hosted by Italy. Forward Edge was sending a mission team to Italy to perform evangelistic dramas at some of the Mondiale venues, and I decided to bring Heather along.

After deplaning in Munich, Heather and I traveled by train to Rome where we joined the rest of the Forward Edge team. Following the 10-day outreach, Heather and I spent several days alone together touring Italy. First, we visited my older sister, Diana, who was then living with her husband, Aldo, and their five children in the coastal town of Manfredonia. We then toured Florence and Venice. Years later, Heather would write to me in a Father's Day card: "I will always remember and appreciate that my first visit to Venice was with a man who will always love me."

The trip to Italy with Heather served as a precedent for future trips with my two younger children, Ryan and Kate. Having decided that 10 was a good age to take my kids on their first mission trips—and with Heather just 14 months Ryan's senior—it wasn't long before Ryan joined me on a trip to Mexico. A missionary friend had invited me to speak at a conference in the city of Leon, and Ry was eager to tag along. My most vivid memory from that trip was a church service in a tiny mountain village. A missionary pilot had flown us to the village, and no sooner had we arrived when Ryan—with his blond hair and blue eyes—became the center of the villagers' attention. Throughout the entire two-hour church service, in fact, every child present had their backs turned toward me and their eyes fixed on Ryan.

When Kate turned 10, it was her turn to travel with me, and the opportunity then available was the most ambitious one yet: *India*. Not surprisingly, Karen had some reservations about Kate traveling to India with me, but I felt confident Kate could handle the trip given her strong constitution, adventuresome spirit, and compassionate heart. I also had a special place in my heart for the Indian subcontinent, and wanted Kate to see and experience it for herself.

And so, for nearly three weeks, Kate would join me on what would become for her the most memorable and, in some ways, most disturbing experience of her childhood. We visited Dharavi,[20] the largest slum in Asia where 600,000 people lived in less than a square mile; toured a "leper town" built with the help of a Christian philanthropist; sat under the stars at a church-run orphanage where each child, one after the other, shared the heartbreaking story of her life; and, to top things off, helped transport two one-year-old orphans from Mumbai to Los Angeles. I will never forget landing at LAX and watching with pride and admiration as Kate—dressed Punjabi-style in tight leggings and a knee-length skirt—delivered the twins into the arms of their adoptive parents. India had been a long, grueling journey for Kate. But if you asked her today "Would you do it again?" I'm confident her answer would be "Yes."

---

20. The academy-award-winning film, *Slumdog Millionaire*, used Dharavi as the location for some of its most heart-wrenching scenes.

Chapter Thirty One

OVER THE NEXT SIX YEARS, FROM 1990 to 1996, God continued to bless the work of Forward Edge. The number of annual mission teams grew, as did our staff and support base. But along with the growth came mounting concerns about our affiliation with Gospel Outreach. From the beginning, Forward Edge had partnered with a broad cross-section of churches throughout the country—Baptist, Presbyterian, Foursquare, and non-denominational. And as time passed, an increasingly smaller percentage of our volunteers came from churches affiliated with GO. With a vision focused solely on extending God's kingdom, Forward Edge no longer seemed to fit within the parameters of a single denomination.

But separating from GO would not be easy. The most daunting challenge was GO's emphasis on what we called "covenant relationships." A person's relationship with GO, we had been taught, was like a marriage—a spiritual union that carried with it the unspoken stricture: "till death do us part." The intent behind the teaching was noble enough. So many followers of Jesus, it seemed, had a hard time committing to a local church—someplace where they could grow to maturity "in the soil where they were planted." Church hopping was epidemic among Christians, in fact…a practice that left many believers weak, disconnected, and of little use to God.

But in the case of GO, "covenant relationships" had become, in my view at least, something of a minimum-security prison. Under no circumstances, it seemed, would leaving GO be equated by its leaders with "God's perfect will." On the contrary, it was looked upon not only with sadness, but intimidating disfavor. This, then, was the challenge that Karen and I now faced.

For more than six months, we had been lifting this challenge to God in prayer. We sought his will in Scripture; met with friends whose counsel we trusted; and tried our best to weigh the reasons for our growing discontent. We battled confusion, double-mindedness and, perhaps more than anything, fear. What if the GO leaders commandeered the ministry of Forward Edge? They had every legal right to do so. And if they did, what would become of my salary? My home? My reputation? The ministry I had worked so hard to nurture and grow?

It was during this season of soul searching that I heard about a conference in Kansas City. The church sponsoring the conference was reputed to be a place where God "showed up" in unique and powerful ways. Intrigued, and desperate for divine direction, I decided to go.

As it turned out, I would spend the week prior to the conference rafting with several friends on the Rogue River in southern Oregon. The trip was exhilarating…and unexpectedly exhausting. I arrived home, on the eve of my departure for Kansas City, at 1:00 in the morning. My flight was at 6:00am.

Sometime between 1:30am and 5:00am, I had a dream. It was the third dream in 20 years (I've told you the other two) that I knew at once was from God. In the dream, I was standing in a house that felt like home. On the first floor of the house, a number of interesting objects were prominently displayed, including a large golden trophy and pictures of well-known people in frames of silver.

And then I was on the second floor of the house: a large empty space with bare walls and not a stick of furniture. Peering through a nearby window, I saw what appeared to be painters standing on a scaffold rolling white paint on the exterior of the house. Their faces were expressionless, and they clearly took no pleasure in their work. Suddenly, one of the painters set down his roller, climbed through the window, and headed straight in my direction. He appeared to be asking me some kind of question, as if I had an answer he was looking for. I mumbled something—something I couldn't understand—and the painter became very excited. "That's it! That's it!" he screamed, falling to the floor and twirling on his back, break-dance style.

Finally, I found myself on the top floor of the house. Three children were sitting in a circle playing some kind of game. They were laughing and having fun, and while there were no adults in the room, I had the overwhelming sense that they were fine, and that everything was just as it should be.

I then arrived at the threshold of a dimly-lit room. Smoke or incense filled the chamber, and I could barely make out a shadowy figure dancing with long silk scarves twirling above her head. I had an almost irresistible urge to enter the room, to join the woman in her dance, to let down my defenses and embrace her... And then I woke up.

What was that about? I gasped, squinting at my alarm clock: 5:15 am. *My flight leaves in less than an hour!* I jumped out of bed, threw some clothes into a suitcase and headed for the Portland airport. Four hours later, I was landing in Kansas City.

Chapter Thirty Two

THE VENUE FOR THE CONFERENCE WAS the Kansas City Convention Center, just twenty minutes from the Kansas City Airport. When I arrived, more than 3,000 people were crammed into the center's cavernous auditorium. A worship band, more gifted than most, was playing an exceptionally anointed version of *I Surrender All*. I felt an extraordinary, almost overwhelming sense of God's presence.

I found a seat near the back of the auditorium and immediately fell to my knees. "I just want your will, God," I cried, still burdened by the challenge I faced with Gospel Outreach. "Just your will...your will...your will..."

At last the worship was over, and a tall, bespectacled man strode confidently to the podium.

"My message today is on worship," he said.

Using as his text Romans 12:1-2, he proceeded to expound on what he called "the true meaning of worship." It was a message I had not only heard before, but expounded on myself a time or two.

"Worship is not music," he declared, a calm authority in his voice. "It's not singing or dancing or clapping our hands. Worship is offering ourselves as living sacrifices to God! This is our reasonable service, the Bible says. And this, and only this, will keep us in the good, pleasing, and perfect will of God."

Suddenly, a wave of emotion swept over me. It was as if I was hearing the message of Romans 12 for the first time. Yes, I'd already surrendered my life to Jesus...more than once. But I was now faced with a new and unique set of circumstances. If I tried to separate Forward Edge from Gospel Outreach, I risked losing everything I held most dear. Was the price tag more than I was willing to pay?

A picture then began to form in my mind. I saw myself walking to the foot of a giant cross, bending down, and placing at the foot of the cross everything I was most afraid of losing: my salary…my reputation…my cherished and carefully-cultivated ministry. I then stood up, turned around, and walked away. I did not look back.

Instantly, I felt an indescribable freedom, as if a giant boulder had been lifted from my shoulders. I had no idea what would come of my decision. But with peace now anchored in my heart, I knew I had nothing to fear.

That night in my hotel room, I took the shower I'd been unable to take earlier in the day. It was here, in the shower, that I received an instantaneous interpretation of my dream about the house. It came to me in a matter of seconds.

The house was my life. The first floor, with its golden trophy and pictures of "well-known people," was symbolic not only of the pressures I'd felt as a child to live up to Dad, but the longing throughout my life to achieve some form of worldly or spiritual "success"…to become—through my own wisdom and strength— "somebody."

The second floor, with its painters masking the house in white, represented my attempts *as a Christian* to appear good, righteous, a spiritual "somebody." And not just my attempts, but those of all people everywhere who thought looking good or cool or accomplished on the outside was more important than the condition and posture of their hearts. I thought of what Jesus told the Pharisees: "You're like whitewashed tombs which indeed appear beautiful outwardly, but inside are full of dead men's bones and all uncleanness" (Matthew 23:27).

And finally, the top floor—with its carefree children and dancing woman—was a picture of what *God* wanted for my life:

childlike trust and intimacy with him. It wasn't pseudo-spirituality, performance, or even good deeds that he wanted from me; it was *a relationship*. Was this the answer that made the stone-faced painter twirl joyfully on his back?[21]

Crocodile tears mingled with water poured down my face as I sobbed uncontrollably in the shower.

I love you, Joseph, came those now familiar words again. *I love you…I love you…I love you.*

---

21. I believe the dancing woman in my dream was a type of the Holy Spirit—one of the three Persons comprising the Triune Christan God—wooing me into a relationship of ever-deepening intimacy.

Chapter Thirty Three

As soon as I returned to Vancouver, I made arrangements to meet with Jim and the other GO elders in Eureka. Two weeks later, fortified by prayer and trusting God for the outcome, I gathered with them in Jim's downtown office.

"I believe God has been speaking to me," I began. "Thank you for taking the time to meet with me. I'll try my best to explain."

For the next 30 minutes, I shared the scriptures, counsel, and personal revelations God had given me over the past few months, including my dream about the house. I then expressed my concerns about Forward Edge's ongoing association with Gospel Outreach.

"I believe God is leading me into a closer, more intimate relationship with him," I concluded. "And this includes trusting him to guide me into his unique plan and purpose for my life."

There was a long pause. Then, as Jim sat silently, each elder expressed their love for me, along with their concerns about Forward Edge becoming disassociated from GO. At last, Jim made a final ruling.

"I believe that *you* believe God is speaking to you, Joe," he said. "And I've always made a point of not standing in the way of an honest man's convictions. You have my blessing, Joe. May the Lord prosper you…and the ministry of Forward Edge."

✳✳✳

From that day onward, God's favor on me, and on Forward Edge, seemed to multiply. The number of volunteers serving on teams grew from less than 200 in 1989 to more than 500 in 1999. In 2000, we sent teams to Kosovo to help widows who'd lost their husbands in the Balkan War. In 2001, we sent volunteers to New York City to minister

MY THREE BEAUTIFUL CHILDREN: RYAN (L),
KATELYN (C), AND HEATHER (R).

to rescue workers at Ground Zero after the 9/11 attack. And in 2005, FEI teams journeyed to Sri Lanka to help build homes for victims of the Indian Ocean Tsunami. Later in 2005, a Portland, Oregon-based foundation, Mission Increase, awarded Forward Edge a million-dollar matching grant to help victims of Hurricane Katrina—especially the poor and elderly—return to their homes. At this writing, almost 3,000 people have served with FEI in the Gulf Coast, repairing 25 church buildings and more than 300 homes.

My family, too, participated firsthand in the ministry of Forward Edge, and over the years Heather, Ryan and Kate would join me on numerous Forward Edge adventures. In 1991, Ry accompanied me to Romania where we ministered in dreary, state-run orphanages, and in 2001 to New York City where we prayed with firemen at Ground Zero just days after 9/11. Kate served with me on a team to the White Mountain Apache Reservation in Arizona where we conducted a vacation Bible school and painted the homes of widows. She would also spend an entire summer in Central America serving with one of our ministry partners in Belize. While in college, Ryan and Heather joined me on a Forward Edge team to Tibet where we participated in "prayer walks" and distributed tracts to curious monks in remote Tibetan monasteries. And, just months after Hurricane Katrina, Heather and her husband, Hessel, would lead a team of Stanford students to Mississippi where they gutted the homes of families devastated by the storm.

As a father, I had wanted my children to know from a young age that they lived in a world fraught with need. I also wanted to expose them—as carefully and responsibly as I could—to "life outside the bubble of the church." In the words of Scripture, I wanted them to be "*in* the world, but not *of* it." And while Karen and I elected to homeeducate through the eighth grade, we did not shield our kids from the classics of art, music, movies and literature. Years later, I would receive a birthday card from one of my children that included the following sentiment:

"Thank you, Dad, for introducing me to the things that inspired you—travel, books, movies, music. In turn, I was inspired, and developed an appetite to discover that which would inspire me...I love and respect who you are, who you have been, and who you will continue to be in my life."

It was also important to me as a father to give my children the freedom and support they needed to become the unique individuals God had designed them to be. Given my experience as a twin, I was sensitive to the fact that siblings can tend to compete, so I did my best to recognize and affirm each of my children's unique talents, gifts and personality traits. More than anything, I encouraged them to believe that they—like every person—were "God's workmanship, created in Christ Jesus for good works which God prepared in advance for them to do" (Eph. 2:10).

So, how did my children turn out? I'm proud to say, extremely well. Heather was valedictorian and homecoming queen of her 1998 graduating class at Prairie High School in Vancouver, Washington and, at the graduation ceremony, she spoke powerfully about her faith in Christ. After turning down a scholarship to Georgetown, she graduated summa cum laude from the University of Puget Sound in Tacoma, Washington with a degree in English Literature, and was one of only two seniors to speak on graduation weekend. Today, she is the mother of two beautiful children, Audrey Sophia and Evangeline Grace (though she may have more by the time you read this). She is also a gifted writer, an anointed Bible teacher, and an extraordinary mother and wife. You can read her insights on marriage, mothering and contemporary culture on her blog: www.thesmallbeginnings.blogspot.com.

In 2006, Ryan graduated from Portland State University with a degree in English Literature, and at this writing is in his third year at Lewis and Clark Law School in Portland, Oregon. He and a classmate won the 2008 "mock trial competition" at Lewis and Clark, and—once he passes the bar exam (God willing)—he looks forward to advocating for the poor and downtrodden. Always a hard worker, Ryan worked his way through college and law school and, while employed part-time at a local Portland law firm, won his first jury trial in July, 2009 (law students in Oregon can try non-felony cases if they apply for and receive a Temporary Practice Card).

In 2007, Kate graduated magna cum laude from Gordon College in Wenham, Massachusetts with a degree in International Relations. She spent her junior year of college at Oxford University in England, and the following summer served as an intern at the White House. After graduating from Gordon, Kate worked in the West Wing as the Executive Assistant to the Deputy Counsel to the President. Kate's tenure in the White House would make it possible for our family to have a series of surreal experiences. For example, Karen attended the 2007 White House Christmas Party and the 2008 Easter Egg Roll Event; I viewed Washington, D.C.'s 2008 Fourth of July fireworks display from the South Lawn of the White House; and, in November 2008, our entire family met briefly with President Bush behind closed doors in the Oval Office. As we shook hands with the President and exited the Oval Office into the sunlit Rose Garden I distinctly recall asking Karen: *Did that really happen?*

I cannot adequately express how proud I am of my children. After all the struggles I had as a young man finding my way, I'm grateful that my own children have a clearer sense of who they are and where they might be headed in life. Karen and my constant prayer is that they will "run with perseverance the race marked out for [them]" by their Father in heaven (Hebrews 12:1).

MY FAMILY IN THE OVAL OFFICE WITH PRESIDENT
GEORGE W. BUSH, NOVEMBER, 2008.

***

Hurricane Katrina proved to be a watershed moment for the ministry of Forward Edge. In addition to the million dollar matching grant, a large foundation based in Vancouver, Washington, Murdock Charitable Trust, awarded Forward Edge a $300k grant to hire full-time field staff in the Gulf Coast. For the first time in its 22-year history, Forward Edge now had *full-time* missionaries—missionaries who would be free to serve anywhere in the world with Forward Edge once our work in the Gulf Coast was complete. As a consequence, by the fall of 2005, Forward Edge transitioned from a short-term mission agency into a full-blown relief and development organization. We would continue to send short-term volunteers (approximately 1,000 every year), but we would limit the number of destinations, and focus our resources on long-term, sustainable projects with an emphasis on disaster response, health care, and programs for vulnerable children.

Our most ambitious project would unfold in the summer of 2006 when two short-term Forward Edge volunteers, Sam Martin and Dusty Hume, would ask Gloria Sequeira a probing question: "If you could do anything for the girls in La Chureca, what would it be?"

"I would get them out of the dump," Gloria responded. "They have no hope or future there. It breaks my heart to see their suffering."

On returning to the States, Sam told me about his conversation with Gloria, and the vision for *Villa Esperanza* (Village of Hope) was born.

"That's when you came into the picture, Gary." I smiled as we sat in the terminal in Houston waiting for yet another connecting flight to Portland. "Without you—and many others—the Village would never have been possible."

"I guess you're right," Gary said, with characteristic humility. "I guess I'm one of those sleeping firemen who finally woke up!"

We both laughed.

"The story of Forward Edge is very inspiring, Joe," Gary then said. "And I can understand now how you came to be involved. But I'm not sure how your relationship with God relates to Forward Edge. I mean, how does knowing that God loves you relate to all your accomplishments over the years?"

I had to think about Gary's question for a few seconds. For one thing, the words "all your accomplishments" made me uneasy. I was deeply aware that whatever good had come through Forward Edge over the years was the result of God working through the lives of thousands of ordinary people. It had little to do with me. My job had simply been to see where God was working around the world and invite others to join him. If I was faithful and didn't get in the way, he would do the rest.

"I guess I can answer your question like this, Gary," I finally said. "Many years ago I read somewhere about a young seminary student who was born with a birthmark on his face. It was a long, unsightly scar that ran from the top of his forehead to the base of his chin. But in spite of this, the boy was remarkably happy, generous, and free from all self-consciousness. So much so that his roommate finally asked him: 'How did you get like this?'

"'All my life,' the boy explained, 'as far back as I can remember, my dad would tell me how much he loved me. The birthmark, he said, was where the angels had kissed me so that he, my dad, would know I was his son. Every day, in fact, my father would hold me in his arms and tell me how special I was and how much he loved me. After a while, I began to feel sorry for people who weren't born with a birthmark on their face.'

"That's what God has done in my life, Gary. And it's what I believe he wants to do in *every* person's life. He wants us to know how much he loves us. Not just so we can be ourselves, but so we can be set free to reach outside ourselves to love and serve others. This is the message of Christianity, Gary. And it's a message God wants us to express not only with our tongues, but with our lives."

I noticed an appreciative gleam in Gary's eye as I said this.

"Yeah, I think I know what you mean," he said, his green eyes wide and luminous. "I think I know what you mean."

Epilogue

IN THE FALL OF 2008, IN the middle of my interviews with applicants for positions at Forward Edge, Frank invited me to speak at his church in California. The church, The Rock of Roseville, had been planted by Frank in 1998 and had grown in recent years to nearly 2,000 congregants. Each week a member of "The Rock" was invited to share a five-minute version of his or her story. And now Frank had asked me to fly in from Portland to share mine.

"Sure," I said when Frank called to invite me. "I'm not sure I can do it in five minutes. But I'll do my best."

Over the years, Frank's church had partnered with Forward Edge to send several mission teams to various parts of the U.S. and overseas. Now, with the Village of Hope project underway, Frank asked if when I visited to share my story I would meet with Rock congregants about a possible Forward Edge team to Nicaragua. Naturally, I was happy to oblige.

But I was not happy about the timeframe allotted for me to speak. Five minutes? *How could I share my story in five minutes?*

At first I planned to write a summary of my story that I could read in the time allotted. But when I sat down to write this, the end result seemed sterile. *I need to share from my heart*, I concluded. I'll write an outline, but I'm not going to read a carefully-scripted speech.

As it turned out, the busyness of my schedule (I was still trying to fill the positions at FEI and traveling to Nicaragua almost monthly) required that I postpone my visit to The Rock until the spring of 2009. I arrived in California on a warm, cloudless day in mid-April. I was excited, but apprehensive, too. *What if I went longer than five minutes?*

It had been years since my last visit to The Rock, and the church had grown considerably since then. They now had a new facility in downtown Roseville where they hosted six weekly services: one on Thursday, two on Saturday, and three on Sunday. I would be sharing at all six, and since I'd arrived on a Thursday, the first would be taking place that evening.

"Be vulnerable, Joe," Frank had exhorted me during a phone conversation prior to my visit. "We like it when people are *raw*."

That night, Frank and I arrived at the church just before 6:00pm. As Frank parked his SUV across the street from the new facility I was immediately impressed. A two-story building with tall glass doors on the ground floor and thin accent windows on the second, The Rock's new church had the appearance of a private secondary school.

"I'll show you around," Frank said.

We exited the car and approached the building. We were about to enter when a blonde woman who appeared to be in her early thirties approached us from the nearby parking lot.

"Hi, Alice," Frank greeted the woman. "I want you to meet my twin brother, Joe."

As the blonde woman reached out to shake my hand I watched as her eyes darted from me…to Frank…then back to me again.

"Wow…you guys don't look *anything* alike!" she blurted, unable to hide her astonishment.

Some things never change, I thought, as I smiled and shook the woman's hand.

"Joe is sharing his story with us tonight," Frank then said, ignoring the woman's remark. "I think you'll be blessed."

Frank and I now entered the building where a high-octane worship band blared from two huge monitors on either side of the foyer. We crossed the foyer and made our way up carpeted stairs to Frank's office on the second floor. A large room with giant windows overlooking the surrounding neighborhood, the office featured a glass conference-room table, a bookcase with photos of family and friends, and a large LCD monitor. A shovel that had been used at the church's groundbreaking ceremony leaned in a corner between two overstuffed sofas.

I was taking all this in when I noticed on the wall above one of the sofas the room's most surprising accessories: framed black-and-white photos of Dad with Harry Truman, John Kennedy, Lyndon Johnson and Pope Pius XXII. Memories of a hot summer day long ago in Atlantic Highlands flashed across my mind.

"Wow...it's strange to see them hanging in your office, Frank," I said, scanning the photographs. "But I'm glad we can finally feel proud of Dad, aren't you? God's done an amazing work in our hearts."

"Yes," Frank agreed, as we stood side by side staring at the pictures. "I actually look forward to seeing him again someday. God willing."

"Me, too, Frank. Me, too."

"We'd better head downstairs now," Frank added. "The service has already started."

Minutes later, Frank and I entered The Rock's main sanctuary, a dimly-lit room with rows of built-in chairs angled downward like the seats in a state-of-the-art theater. A band of musicians was playing on stage, their images projected on two enormous monitors that hung on either side of the platform. Frank and I sat together in the sanctuary's front row.

When worship was over, and after a few brief announcements, Frank stepped to the podium to introduce me.

"I'm thrilled to have my twin brother here tonight," he said, a genuine warmth in his voice. "He's going to be sharing his story with us, and I know you'll find it fascinating. Before that, though, we're going to show a brief video about a project that Joe's ministry has undertaken in Nicaragua. I think you'll find it interesting."

The lights now dimmed, and images of the Managua landfill

appeared on the sanctuary's monitors. The video clip was an excerpt from an Emmy-award-winning documentary which had aired on Portland TV the previous Thanksgiving and Christmas Eve. When the video ended, Frank returned to the podium and invited me to join him on the platform.

"I'm so proud of my brother," he said, his voice slightly cracking. "I hope you'll open your hearts to him now as he comes to tell us his story."

I stood silent for a moment, alone on the platform, looking out at hundreds of faces that seemed to glow with anticipation.

Just keep it real, Joe, I said to myself. *And leave the rest to God.*

"I had two major struggles growing up," I began. "One was the pressure I felt to achieve some form of worldly success. The other was the feeling I had of being small…second-rate…not good enough. I didn't realize at the time that these feelings were not unique to me. They're what most people feel at some point or other in their lives…if their being honest at least."

Conscious of my miniscule time limit, I now hurried through several scenes that personified my opening statement: Frank and me hanging Dad's photos on the walls of our New Jersey den; the day of our First Communion; and my performance of JFK's speech in Florida.

"I was determined to prove myself," I explained, "to live up to my father, to create a 'persona' that would somehow earn me the love and approval I craved."

I then summarized my post-college years: my dropping out to California, my overland journey to India, and my quest for spiritual answers.

"As I look back on those years," I said, "I can see that even though I thought of myself as 'a seeker,' it was God who was seeking *me*."

I then shared about my visit to Smartsville after Frank's conversion; Jerry Russell flagging down our school bus on the outskirts of

Sacramento; Sabine sharing her story at Table Mountain; and the tract-distributing Christians on the border of India and Pakistan.

I now glanced at the clock at the back of the sanctuary. *I'd been speaking for ten minutes!* I can't stop now, I thought. I pressed on.

I shared about my vision of the cross in Delhi; the Brooklyn longshoreman telling me to "get auf my trip;" and my experience of God loving me in the prayer room at Oxford Street.

"I stand before you tonight a free man," I proclaimed at last. "By a miracle of God's grace, I am *free*...free to be the flawed but useful person God made me...free to love...to serve...to make some small but needed contribution to God's purposes in the earth.

"Thank you for listening," I concluded. "That is my story."

No sooner had I said this than the entire congregation rose to their feet and engulfed me in steady applause. I'd been speaking for fifteen minutes, but all sense of time had vanished from me now, And from everyone else, too, it seemed.

Slowly, Frank moved from his seat and climbed the steps that led to the platform. I could now see that tears were rolling down his cheeks and that his lower lip was quivering.

"I love you, Joe," he whispered in my ear as we embraced.

"I love you, too, Frank," I whispered. "I love you, too."

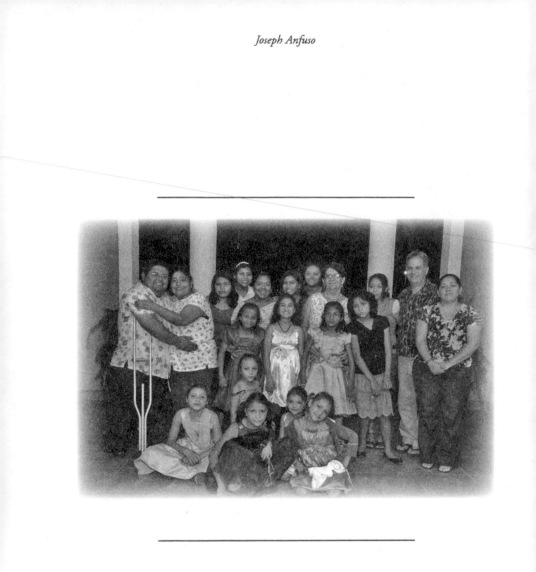

FIFTEEN OF THE FIRST SIXTEEN GIRLS AT *VILLA*
ESPERANZA, WITH THEIR HOUSE MOMS, SANDRA
(R.) AND MAMA ALBA (FIFTH FROM R.). JOE
ANFUSO IS SECOND FROM THE RIGHT; WILBERT
AND GLORIA ARE ON THE FAR LEFT.

GARY ECKELMAN went on to design the Village of Hope, which is now home to 32 girls from La Chureca. He also designed another children's home and a surgery center/medical clinic in Puerto Cabezas on Nicaragua's Atlantic Coast. Today, he serves on Forward Edge International's Board of Directors.

FRANCIS ANFUSO is the senior pastor of The Rock of Roseville in Roseville, California. He is the author of three books, *Perfectly Positioned, Father Wounds,* and *2029/Church of the Future.*

JOSEPH ANFUSO, and his twin brother, Francis, turned 60 on February 23, 2009. On his birthday, Joe received a phone call from the girls at Villa Esperanza. They sang Happy Birthday to him in Spanish. It was the best birthday present of his life.

Acknowledgements

I have so many people to thank. First and foremost, my wife, Karen, who typed and re-typed the earliest versions of this book in the late 1970s, who helped me believe it would one day get published, and who was always the first to read whatever I wrote along the way. Virginia Muir who "planted the seed" for an autobiography back in 1977. Peter Gilquist and Roy Carlisle who gave me their honest and knowledgeable advice. Dave Hazard who tried, all those years ago, to get me to do what I wasn't ready or able to do at the time. Marie Prys for her expert editing of the current manuscript. Charles Chesnut for listening to my vision for the cover and making it a reality. My siblings—Francis, Maria, Victor and Diana—for their positive feedback, and their help in getting the details right. Pam Lagielski, Katy Crane, and Carma Roetsicender for their proofreading and heartfelt encouragement. Kam and Lisa Delashmut, and Dean and Cindy McGregor, for making their beautiful homes available to me so I could get away to write. Brad Fenison, who saw merit in my story, and who, with the help of his son, Chris, brought this book to print. And most of all, the living God of the Bible, who persistently drew me to Himself, and who continues to write the story of my life.